The Blood Speaks

DISCOVER THE LIFE-GIVING POWER OF JESUS' SACRIFICE

by
Larry Huggins

Harrison House
Tulsa, Oklahoma

06 05 04 03   10 9 8 7 6 5 4 3 2 1

The Blood Speaks—
Discover the Life-Giving Power of Jesus' Sacrifice
ISBN 1-57794-422-4
Copyright © 2003 by Larry Huggins
P.O. Box 140645
Austin, TX 78714-0645 USA

Published by Harrison House, Inc.
P.O. Box 35035
Tulsa, Oklahoma 74153

Contents

Foreword

It is a dynamic truth that the life of the flesh is in the blood. (Lev. 17:11.) This is true of spiritual life as well as natural life. If the blood ceases to flow to any organ of our body, that part of the body will die. Spiritually, no one can see heaven without the blood of the sacrifice.

Almost every special event in the Bible is related to some extent with the blood. This association began in the Garden of Eden with the sacrifice of two innocent animals to atone for Adam and Eve's rebellion and transgression.

In these last days, this subject is disdained by some and adored by others according to their personal relationship with God.

All of us can appreciate the labors of Larry Huggins in producing this book. Indeed, *The Blood Speaks* to the total population of earth today.

May God bless you as you study this book!

Lester Sumrall
South Bend, Indiana

Introduction

This book is about the divine life that's in the blood of Jesus. Admirable books touch on the blood covenant and the legal side of redemption. This book discusses the vital side of redemption.

In the blood of Jesus there is a divine materiality, an actual, heavenly substance. It is the very essence of immortality.

According to the Word of God, God raised Jesus from the dead through the blood of the everlasting covenant (Heb. 13:20), which was Jesus' own blood. Yes, there is something in the blood of Jesus that has the power to raise the dead, heal the sick, and wash away sin so thoroughly that even God cannot find the stain. There is something in the blood of Jesus that evil spirits cannot tolerate (Col. 1:20; 2:15) and that speaks to God as well as to the heart of man. His blood says, *I am the light that illuminates every man. In Me there is no weakness, no failure, no lack, but only life, happiness, and immortality.*

Please read this book with an open Bible. See for yourself what the Word of God says. The Bible is the final authority.

I also encourage you to read this book with an open mind. Words paint pictures. If you allow yourself to read without reservation, the visuals will come alive. This is not just a book of ideas, but of indelible images.

Finally, read this book with an open heart. It is, above all, a book of inspiration and revelation. *The Blood Speaks* isn't organized like a motivational manual. However, with the Holy Spirit's help, you will be a different person by the time you turn the last page.

As you read, please listen with your heart. Hear what the blood of Jesus is saying to the heavenly Father. Then you will begin to understand His fathomless love for you. *The Blood Speaks* for you now!

A Word About the Second Edition

When this information was first published in 1980, someone who was quite excited about *The Blood Speaks,* asked me if I had plans to release another book. He was surprised by my answer, *"Not for a long time I hope."* Then I explained that some books do not pass the test of time.

As it turns out, this book has blessed tens of thousands of people for over two decades now. When I hear people refer to it as a classic, I know it's because of the significance of the subject, not necessarily the skill of the writer.

When I am told that people have read it repeatedly, I know something is speaking to the reader's heart. I must never silence that voice. In this second edition, I hope I have amplified it.

Until now, this book has been changed only slightly, from one printing to the next, and those changes did not call for a new edition. However, the addition of an entirely new chapter, "What the Blood Says About You," does warrant a new edition. This edition retains the compelling content of the previous versions, with only slight improvements for readability.

Even now, this work is not intended to be an exhaustive description of the subject. It is merely a snapshot of Glory.

2 PETER 1:19-21

19 We have also a more sure word of prophecy; whereunto ye do well that ye take heed, as unto a light that shineth in a dark place, until the day dawn, and the day star arise in your hearts:

20 Knowing this first, that no prophecy of the scripture is of any private interpretation.

21 For the prophecy came not in old time by the will of man: but holy men of God spake as they were moved by the Holy Ghost.

CHAPTER 1

A Life of Health

Let's begin at the beginning. The problem with humanity is bad blood. For thousands of years, since the fall of Adam and Eve in the Garden of Eden, mankind's blood has been polluted by sin. Sickness came upon mankind and entered the world of human experience because of sin.

On the other hand, spiritual wholeness and divine health comes by the blood of Jesus. Divine health is the birthright of every born-again child of God. It is a benefit of being in union with God through Jesus Christ.

THREE DEGREES OF DIVINE HEALTH

I have heard it taught that John G. Lake observed there are three degrees (or levels) of divine health.

The first degree is divine healing. This is when you are sick and through prayer and faith you are healed. The second degree is divine health. This means that you don't need to be healed because you don't get sick; you simply walk continuously in divine health. That is better than constantly needing healing.

I want to make it clear here that no one should ever look down upon anyone who has physical problems. As members of the body of Christ, our job is to help one another—to weep with those that weep, to rejoice with those that rejoice. (Rom. 12:15.) Remember, when one suffers, we all suffer. (1 Cor. 12:26.)

Likewise, you should never feel condemned if you find you have a need to be healed. No one starts out as a full-grown person in the natural, and no one starts out as a full-grown Christian spiritually. (See Eph. 4:13.) Give yourself time to grow in faith.

With that said, the third degree of divine health, according to the teaching I heard, is what John G. Lake called divine life. There is a place in Christ where we can walk in actual divine life. Divine life is Jesus living His life through a child of God, unhindered. We can walk just like Jesus walked when He was upon the earth—healing the sick and raising the dead. In fact, we are commanded in the Bible to do it. (Matt. 10:8; Mark 16:17,18.)

Divine life should be our highest goal. God's highest and best for us is to walk 100 percent of the time in the life, love, and power of God.

Early in my walk with God, I came across a passage of Scripture that has become very dear to me:

EZEKIEL 16:4-6

4   And as for thy nativity, in the day thou wast born thy navel was not cut, neither wast thou washed in water to supple thee; thou wast not salted at all, nor swaddled at all.

5   None eye pitied thee, to do any of these unto thee, to have compassion upon thee; but thou wast cast out in the open field, to the loathing of thy person, in the day that thou wast born.

6   And when I passed by thee, and saw thee polluted in thine own blood, I said unto thee when thou wast in thy blood, Live; yea, I said unto thee when thou wast in thy blood, Live.

These verses describe my personal experience with the Lord and apply to all believers, everywhere. It is a picture of God and Israel, with Israel being a type, or symbol, of the church of Jesus Christ. God said to her, "When I passed by thee, and saw thee polluted in thine own blood, I said unto thee...Live" (v. 6).

Israel was like a child who was born out of due season and abandoned, left to fend for herself, covered in filth, bleeding to death and helpless. But God, passing by, saw her polluted in her own blood, and cried to her, *"Live!"*

This is a powerful blood-related scripture. I have used it many times to minister healing to people with various blood disorders. I have also used it to stop bleeding. It is a powerful truth that will work for those who understand it.

Once, at a church in Tennessee, a talented young lady approached me for prayer. Before she could tell me what her problem was, I said by the Spirit, *"You may not know it, but you have a blood disorder."* Sadly, this beautiful, young psalmist's face was severely blemished by acute acne. I spoke Ezekiel 16:6 over her.

The following year I returned to her home church. She had asked her pastor for permission to sing a special song and give her personal testimony. Her face seemed to glow as she praised God, saying, "Last year Brother Huggins said I had a blood disorder. I have seen many dermatologists and undergone every kind of treatment, but nothing helped. No one had ever correctly diagnosed my problem as a blood disorder. Since Rev. Huggins ministered to me, the acne has gone away completely, and even the scars are disappearing!"

In another incident, a young man who was visiting our fellowship came in just before the Sunday service began. As he was walking toward the sanctuary, he suddenly had a violent, epileptic seizure. As he fell, his feet kicked out from under him, his head hit the floor hard, and his scalp split. He was lying there, helpless, convulsing and bleeding in the foyer of the church.

The people standing nearby seemed stunned and incapable of helping him. However, one of the believers in the church, passing by at that moment, knew about Ezekiel 16:6 and said in a firm voice, "When I passed by thee, and saw thee polluted in thine own blood, I said unto thee when thou wast in thy blood, Live." The bleeding stopped instantly!

Those standing nearby were impressed by this demonstration of God's healing power. They had witnessed the efficacy of Ezekiel 16:6.

I once preached to a large crowd in Oklahoma. A young woman in the congregation jumped up, held her nose tightly, and ran out of the service. Her nose was bleeding. I looked up, understood her situation, and without hesitation quoted Ezekiel 16:6.

She continued towards the bathroom, and I kept on preaching without explaining what had just happened. The people in the congregation must have thought I had just thrown that verse in unexpectedly. Actually, I had directed my words toward the young woman with the bleeding nose.

After the service the young lady came to me and said, "Brother Huggins, I get nosebleeds quite frequently. They are usually an ordeal because it is so hard to get them stopped. Tonight, when I felt it starting, I put pressure on it and ran from the service. I didn't want to draw attention to myself. However, as I was running from the service I heard you quote that scripture. At first, I didn't realize you were referring to me. One of my girlfriends told me afterwards that you actually pointed your finger at me. This is extraordinary, but by the time I was halfway to the ladies' restroom, I noticed that my nose had stopped bleeding."

I replied, "Yes, I know. To my knowledge, Ezekiel 16:6 works every time, if you believe it."

HEALING IS IN THE ATONEMENT

In Peter's first epistle, we read these words pertaining to Jesus:

1 PETER 2:24

24 Who his own self bare our sins in his own body on the tree, that we, being dead to sins, should live unto righteousness: *by whose stripes ye were healed.*

In the very same verse we see that Jesus died for our sins and for our physical sicknesses. Healing is in the atonement. Our salvation is a total salvation—spirit, soul, and body.

Peter quoted from Isaiah 53:5, which you may have committed to memory: "He was wounded for our transgressions, he was bruised for our iniquities: the chastisement of our peace was upon him; and with his stripes we are healed."

Thank God for the wounds that Jesus bore. It was by His stripes, or lacerations, that He bought and paid for our healing. He secured our right to live in divine health and our right to ultimately walk in divine life.

We learn from Bible scholars that Jesus was beaten with a whip made of leather thongs with sharp pieces of bone or lead, which weighted the thongs and tore the flesh. This was the type of "scourge" the Romans used in Jesus' day.[1]

According to W. E. Vine, the Jewish method of "scourging" was 13 stripes on the breast and each shoulder.[2] Jesus was raked 39 times with a three-stranded whip that had bits of bone and metal woven into it. That adds up to at least 117, cruel lacerations across Jesus' chest and shoulders. I have heard people speculate that there were perhaps 350 lashes laid upon Him! I cannot verify that number, but I do know that Jesus was wounded for the total healing of every category of disease. (Ps. 103:3.)

Today doctors are still discovering diseases: AIDS, Legionnaires' disease, swine flu, toxic shock syndrome, Hong Kong flu, to name a few. However, I unequivocally believe that Jesus bore stripes in His body for all disease: new or old, known or unknown.

It is one thing to believe something works. It's another thing to understand *why* it works. We Christians are instructed to have an answer whenever we are questioned about our faith. (1 Peter 3:15.) Some simply believe things because it's their church creed or their family tradition. That is not good enough. We should have a biblical basis for each of our beliefs.

There is an old story about a young husband who noticed that his new bride had just cut off the ends of a ham before she baked it. When he asked why she did it, her answer was, "That's how my mother always baked a ham. She always cut off the ends."

"Oh, really?" replied the curious husband. "And why did your mother cut off the ends of the ham?"

"Well, I don't know," she said. "I'll call and ask her." "Hello, Mom! I'm cooking a ham, and I'd like to know why you always cut off the ends of your hams."

"Oh," Mom answered, "that's because your grandmother always did it that way, and I learned to cook from her."

The young wife decided to call her grandmother and find out why she always cut off the ends of the ham. Grandmother cleared up the mystery, "Well, when I was young, I had a very small roasting pan. I couldn't fit a whole ham into it, so I always cut off the ends!"

This humorous story illustrates how traditions can get started and then take on an air of authority. Jesus said religious traditions *void* the power of God, "[the authority of] the Word of God" (Mark 7:13 AMP).

We believers often quote 1 Peter 2:24, "…by whose [Christ's] stripes ye were healed," as our personal confession of healing: *By His stripes I am healed.* We meditate on it. If we were healed, then we are healed! And if we are healed, then we are not sick. We are simply not going to give in to symptoms! We must choose to believe the Bible over our feelings and give first place to God's Word: By His stripes we are healed.

If you need healing, take hold of the promise and receive your miracle. Make the irrevocable decision that you are going to walk in divine health. If sickness comes to your house, it will see a "No Vacancy" sign. As a believer, you are filled with God and His Word. Continue to fill your spirit with more of His Word, and inevitably you will walk in divine life! That is faith, and faith pleases God!

HEALTH IS IN THE BLOOD

Again, Ezekiel 16:6 says, "And when I passed by thee, and saw thee polluted in thine own blood, I said unto thee when thou wast in thy blood, Live...." In the natural realm, your ability to resist disease depends primarily upon the health of your blood. I am not a physician, but I remember from grade school that when we nick our skin, our bloodstream immediately circulates coagulants to stop the bleeding and white corpuscles to combat infection. The blood rushes oxygen and nutrients to the wound to rebuild injured cells.

Surgeons take care to reattach severed blood vessels so the tissues will receive an adequate supply of blood. Otherwise the tissues will die. Healing is in the blood. If the blood isn't healthy, the body isn't healthy. Without healthy blood there can be no lasting health.

Some time ago I went to India for a crusade. I had not planned to take the trip to India but had arranged for another man of God to go. However, at the last minute, he could not go. That meant I had to quickly change my plans and go in his place.

When I left the United States, I was already close to exhaustion, having just completed six weeks, non-stop, on the road. To be perfectly honest, I hadn't been eating, sleeping, or even praying right! Nevertheless, I just took my belt in another notch and headed off to India! When I finally arrived in India, I was too busy to sleep well. I didn't eat well. It rained constantly, and I got wet, then dry, then wet again. If you have never been to this area of the world, take my word for it, under the best of conditions it can tax your immune system.

While there, I contracted a rare virus in my blood and became extremely ill. I was so sick that I could hardly pray. All I could do was groan. I was exhausted, lonely, lying on a rope cot 14,000 miles from home, freezing one moment and burning up the next. My clothes and bed sheets were wet with sweat, and I hurt all over. The symptoms were very painful, like the flu, but worse.

The Christians in India prayed for me, but eventually they became alarmed by my condition and took me to an old, poorly equipped hospital. The Indian doctor gave me some out-of-date penicillin.

To no surprise, it was ineffective. I had a viral infection. I am a tough soldier, so I stayed until the end of my crusade. I would preach and then turn the service over to the altar workers. They would pray for the people, and I would bundle up in my overcoat, go back to my cold, damp room and lie there, shaking until dawn. I was fighting for my life. The devil was out to kill me. All I could utter was, "Devil, you're not going to kill me. I am going to recover." When I finally got back to the United States, after a sleepless, thirty-six hour journey, I looked half-dead. I was weak and pale. There was no strength in my limbs. If I pushed my finger into my skin, the skin wouldn't push back. I was dehydrated, had low blood pressure, and my eyes were sunken into my head. My temperature was subnormal, and I ached all over.

As soon as I arrived home, I went to see a Christian doctor. After examining me, he said, "You have a rare viral infection in your blood. In fact, I recently lost an otherwise healthy forty-year-old patient with a similar infection."

"What can you do for me?" I asked.

"Nothing," he said. "You just have to have faith in God."

I can tell you, if you wait until you need faith before you get faith, you're almost too late.

He said, "Your white blood cell count is so low that you don't have any resistance to disease. You could catch another infection and complicate matters. What you need to do is go home, rest in bed for at least a month, drink plenty of fluids, study, and pray."

I followed the doctor's orders, but I must admit I didn't do it a whole month. I spent two weeks in bed, flat on my back, resting and praying. My medicine was lots of rest, lots of water, and lots of faith confessions of, "By His stripes I was healed."

Later a pathologist who heard about my case told me it was a miracle that I didn't die. He said my condition was incurable.

I was cured by faith in the power of the blood that flowed from the stripes of Jesus.

The devil had boasted, "I'm going to kill you! That will teach you to come to India preaching the gospel!"

I recovered because I took the doctor's advice, rested, read the Word, and prayed. I built up my blood and my faith by mediating on God's Word.

On my next trip to India, there were huge crowds in my crusade. Thousands of them were saved and hundreds were healed! At the writing of this book, I have held fifteen miracle crusades in India.

YOUR LIFE IS IN THE BLOOD

The life of all flesh is in the blood. In Leviticus 17:11 God tells us: "For the life of the flesh is in the blood...." The only life that flesh has is the life it gets from the blood.

Blood is a unique, living substance. It is not like the other fluids in our bodies, such as tears. Those secretions are merely organic compounds, but blood is actually liquid, living tissue![3] When the blood supply is cut off, the flesh dies. Without blood there is no life. It is that simple.

When I was a small child, I put a rubber band around my finger and caused my finger to turn blue. It frightened my mother. "Take that rubber band off your finger! Do you want your finger to fall off?" That scared me, but she was right. If I had left it on, the flesh of my finger would have eventually died without the circulation of blood.

Blood travels from the heart, through the arteries, into the capillaries, and back through the veins to the heart, making two complete cycles every sixty seconds. The systemic cycle travels to the far reaches of the body in about thirty seconds![4] That seems amazing to me. That means if a main artery were severed, you could bleed to death in seconds. When the apostle Paul was preaching to the Athenians about "THE UNKNOWN GOD" (Acts 17:23), he said, God "...hath made of *one blood* all nations of men for to dwell on all the face of the earth, and hath determined the times before appointed, and the bounds of their habitation" (v. 26).

The Amplified Bible says, "...one [common origin, one source, one blood]...." All men derive their bloodline from one common ancestor. That common source is Adam, the first man. The Hebrew word ADAM, is from a word that means "to show blood" (as "in the face"), "ruddy i.e. a human being," ("an individual" or "the species, mankind").[5]

GOD'S FIRST MAN

In the first chapter of John, John is speaking of Jesus, the "Word" who existed from the beginning, prior to Adam's creation, but came to earth as the Second Adam, the Word made flesh.

JOHN 1:1–5,9

1   *In the beginning was the Word, and the Word was with God, and the Word was God.*

2   The same was in the beginning with God.

3   All things were made by him; and without him was not any thing made that was made.

4   In him was life; and the life was the light of men.

5   And the light shineth in darkness; and the darkness comprehended it not....

9   That was the true Light, which lighteth every man that cometh into the world.

God is life.[6] He gave the initial spark of life, biological life, which animates every person who has ever lived. Life didn't begin from lightning striking swamp ooze or from cosmic rays. Acts 17:28 says, "In him we live, and move, and have our being...."

Everyone's "light" was lit by God, and He made all men—of all nations—of one common origin, Adam. There is no biblical basis for racism. Biologically all people are the same. Our common denominator is blood. It is commonly accepted that all human beings have a common ancestor. We know from reading the Word of God that every man's DNA goes back to Adam and Eve.

ACTS 17:26 (NIV)

26   From one man he made every nation of men, that they should inhabit the whole earth....

GENESIS 3:20

20 And Adam called his wife's name Eve; because she was the mother of all living.

GENESIS 1:26,27

26 And God said, Let us make man in our image, after our like-ness: and let them have dominion over the fish of the sea, and over the fowl of the air, and over the cattle, and over all the earth, and over every creeping thing that creepeth upon the earth.

27 So God created man in his own image, in the image of God created he him; male and female created he them.

The life that Adam and Eve had was the life God gave them. He made them in His image. This is hard for religious people to grasp, but initially, Adam and Eve had exactly the same quality of life and the same quality of being as God.

This is more fully explained in the second chapter of Genesis:

GENESIS 2:7

7 And the LORD God formed man of the dust of the ground, and breathed into his nostrils the breath of life....

The reason man needed to be redeemed was sin. The Bible says that because of Adam's transgression, all men became sinners. (1 Cor. 15:21,22.) But it also says that if through the First Adam all men were made sinners and all men die, then through the Second Adam [Jesus] all men will be made alive. (1 Cor. 15:45–47.)

What are the differences between the First Adam and the Second Adam? More importantly, what are the similarities between the First Adam and the Second Adam? Have you considered the quality of life that Adam and Jesus had in common?

God formed Adam from the dust of the ground, elemental particles, and created his physical body. At this time it was just a body, inert and lifeless.

Likewise, God also created a body for Jesus. In Hebrews 10:5 Jesus is quoted as saying prophetically to God, "Sacrifice and offering thou wouldest not, but a body hast thou prepared me." His body was prepared for Him. The life of all flesh is in the blood, not just in the body. When Adam was first created, he had no life. He was merely dust formed into a body, until God breathed life into him. The life of God went directly into the first man's blood.

God took Adam, a lifeless form, mute, cold, and breathed into his lifeless nostrils the breath of life. The same life that God had on the inside of Himself was imparted into Adam's blood particles.

The most intimate correspondence between the blood and the outside world is breath. Oxygen goes directly into the bloodstream by way of the lungs. Then through a remarkable process, oxygen diffuses through the capillary walls from the lungs into the blood. The oxygen cycles throughout the body and waste gasses are exhaled. This cycle, when completed, cleanses the blood and recharges it with oxygen.

Adam, at his inception, had no life in his blood. His blood-fluid was inert. Then God breathed into his lungs the breath of life. Immediately Adam's blood became charged with life. His heart, touched by divine life, began to beat. It picked up the heavenly substance that came from God's breath and began pumping it throughout his bloodstream. In a matter of seconds Adam was totally alive!

Adam was a God-class of being. He walked upon the earth with God's life resident in his blood![7] *The life is in the blood.*

CHAPTER 2

From Life to Death

Adam had divine life pumping through his veins. He had the nature of God, life-eternal, resident in His bloodstream. He had the luminous love of God flowing through his being.

God is good. He is the Author of every good gift and every perfect gift. (James 1:17.) Adam had heaven's pure, wholesome goodness pumping through his veins. God never intended for Adam, or mankind for that matter, to know sickness or suffer death. God intended for Adam, and mankind, to have the same quality of life that He had.

In the beginning, divine life was resident in Adam's blood. Adam's sin was of the highest magnitude. He deliberately turned his back on God and made Satan his lord. He committed the damnable act of supreme treason and sold himself and humanity into the slavery of sin.

It was the reverse of being born again. When a person is born again, God's Spirit and nature, which is life, enters him. Adam allowed the nature of Satan, which is death, to enter him. When death came *in,* divine life went out. All that was left was biological life vulnerable to disease and physical death. Living apart from God in the flesh is not really living.

When sin was conceived, Adam was cursed. His nature changed and his blood was polluted with sin. He had bad blood, and because Adam was the progenitor of all humanity, his sin passed upon all men, even over them who had not sinned after the similitude of Adam's transgression. (Rom. 5:14.)

People do not need to be taught how to sin. From the time of man's fall, sin has dominated human society. Man's problem isn't that he is immoral. That is a symptom. His problem is polluted blood. The consequences were physical as well as spiritual.[1]

It has been said that small children are not held responsible for their actions until they reach, what some call, the age of accountability. Eventually, sin will spoil their innocence. They don't have to be taught how to sin. They do it spontaneously.

However, children do need to be taught how not to sin. Here is a sober truth. Even civilized people, who by self-control and discipline manage to behave decently and morally, are still doomed because their very nature is wrong.

This is hard for some people to grasp, but sin is a spiritual disease. It is my opinion that sin is actually a hereditary blood disease. It's a family curse passed from Adam to the whole human race, even to those who had not sinned in the same way as Adam.[2] The whole human race was, *and is*, infected with sin. There is only one cure, inoculation with the blood of Jesus!

Sin was such a problem in Noah's day that God repented for having made mankind. He told Noah, "...The end of all flesh is come before me; for the earth is filled with violence through them; and, behold, I will destroy them with the earth" (Gen. 6:13).

The sin-disease was so terrible that humanity had to be destroyed like a herd of anthrax-infected cattle. However, one man, Noah, and his family were spared. The Bible says, "Noah *found grace in the eyes of the LORD*" (v. 8). God spared Noah and his family because he was a preacher of righteousness. God saw hope in Noah, but sin demanded the balance of humanity to be eradicated. A great flood came upon the earth, putting an end to critically contaminated humanity.

Perhaps, by slowing the proliferation of the sin-plague, God could bring about His plan of redemption *before* reaching the point of diminishing returns. God would begin again through Noah's bloodline.

Looking back for a moment to the outbreak of sin, notice how wickedness passed to Adam's offspring. Among their other children, Eve bore Adam two sons, Cain and Abel. Sin rose up and Cain murdered his brother, Abel. There is only one explanation for it—sin!

Sin was lying dormant in Abel and Cain's blood. God warned Cain of the consequences of activating it: "If thou doest well, shalt thou not be accepted? and if thou doest not well, sin lieth at the door…" (Gen. 4:7). Do you see that? Cain yielded to sin, and it manifested in fratricide; he murdered his brother. It could have occurred the other way; Able could have murdered Cain. Sin is indiscriminate.

I am sure Cain seemed and looked normal, but one day, something rose up within him. Sin had been there all along, dormant, but inevitably it manifested as envy and betrayal.

Cain's crime couldn't be blamed upon society or his environment. He had bad blood. Bringing offerings to God didn't make him good. Religion didn't make him good. He still had evil in his heart. Mere religion may change man's outside, but only the blood of Jesus can cleanse a man's sinful heart.[3] Only God can change man's nature.

In the beginning, Adam was created to live forever, but after the curse of sin entered his blood, he lived only a few short years—"nine hundred and thirty."[4] Certainly, nine hundred years seems like a long time to us today; but when compared to the eternity Adam was scheduled to live, it was nothing. Something in his blood robbed him of eternal life. That something was death. His blood carried spiritual death. Physical death is the byproduct of sin.

FROM LIFE TO DEATH

It is only through providence that the human race survives. Sinful men are fragile. They exist, balanced on the edge of a razor, teetering between heaven and hell. Had God not intervened, humanity would have self-destructed long ago.

Man's sin nature drives him toward destruction. It may lie dormant for a while, but inevitably it rises up again, just like that blood disease I contracted in India.

After my initial recovery, for the next six months, every time I would get the least bit tired the symptoms would try to come back after I preached for an hour. I could feel it in my blood. I continued to curse the symptoms and praise God for my healing. One day it was utterly gone. Don't ask me why it took so long. I don't know. I am just glad it is gone.

So it is with unregenerate man. He tries to be moral. He tries to behave in a civilized manner and suppress his sinful nature but, inevitably, sin rises up out of him, sometimes merely disappointing, but often frightening and horrible.

I read about a man who was bathing his small son. This was just an ordinary suburban father, respected and a member of the PTA, as I recall. As he was playfully giving his toddler son a bath, *something* rose up in him and provoked him to forcefully hold his helpless child under the water until he drowned. Coming to his senses the father screamed, "Oh, God, no! What have I done? WHAT HAVE I DONE!"

Hearing his shrieks, his wife rushed into the bathroom. When she saw what he had done, she cried, "Oh, my God! What have you done? How could you do this?"

"I don't know," the man wept. "I don't know. Something just came over me!"

Later he told the police, "I don't know what came over me. I don't do things like this. I'm not that kind of person. I'm not a criminal. I'm a family man. I have a good job. I love my son. Can you tell me what's in me that would make me kill my own little boy?" They had no answer.

I can answer his question. There is something in man, innate, sinister like spores of death lurking in his blood, compelling him to sin. The only hope for anyone is a transfusion of uncontaminated, sinless blood.

Society doesn't need more law or more religion. It's not a morality issue but a sin issue. So-called civilized people are just as sinful as barbarians. Sin is no respecter of persons.

Until man's heart changes, society will continue building more prisons. Frankly, without revival, anarchy is inevitable. Religion is not the cure. Neither is attending church or calling oneself a Christian. New life is the only answer. Uncontaminated life is available only through the blood of Jesus, the Second Adam. God had to inoculate humanity with his very life and nature. He sent His life down from heaven, in the blood of His incarnate Son, so life could again flow into the human bloodline. The moment you accept Christ into your life, His life begins to flow into you that gives new *meaning to believing God with your whole heart.* Get God's life into your blood!

THE BLOOD IN JESUS' VEINS

God had a foolproof strategy for bypassing the tainted blood of Adam and getting heaven's anointed blood back on the earth. A virgin named Mary found favor in the sight of God. An angel appeared to her saying:

LUKE 1:28,35

28 ...Hail, thou that art highly favoured, the Lord is with thee: blessed art thou among women....

35 ...The Holy Ghost shall come upon thee, and the power of the Highest shall overshadow thee: therefore also that holy thing which shall be born of thee shall be called the Son of God.

Today, skeptics and secularist-theologians cast doubt on the virgin birth. Consider the significance of the virgin birth. Because Mary had not intimately known a man, there was no way the fetus, planted in Mary's womb by God, could have had tainted, Adamic blood.

As you know, conception occurs when the female ovum is united with the male sperm. Only after fertilization does life and embryonic growth commence. Cardiovascular development occurs soon after fertilization. Without fertilization there could be no blood.

A simple experiment proves this. Perhaps your science teacher demonstrated this to you. It requires two eggs, one fertile and one unfertile, and a strong light source. Unfertilized eggs are what you usually buy at the grocery store.

Incubate both eggs for a while. Shine the light through the unfertilized egg and you will not see any blood. An unfertilized chicken egg has no blood in it.

After just a few hours of incubation, you can hold a fertilized chicken egg up in front of a strong light and see the little veins of blood that have begun to grow. Only a fertilized egg has blood in it.

Mary was unfertilized; meaning, she didn't know a man in the biblical sense. She conceived the Son of God by the overshadowing of the Holy Spirit. The Virgin Birth produced a human being with sin-free blood that was not of Adamic origin.

Yet Christ did have blood, did He not? Therefore some form of fertilization must have taken place. Oh, yes! She was impregnated by the Word of God through the Holy Spirit.

JOHN 1:14

14 And the Word was made flesh, and dwelt among us, (and we beheld his glory, the glory as of the only begotten of the Father,) full of grace and truth.

Let's review before we carry this further. In the human fetus, as in the chicken embryo, no blood can develop without fertilization. The mother does not give her blood to the baby. The blood is developed only after the male fertilizes the egg, at conception. Without a male involved, there would be no fetus and, therefore, no blood.

Therefore, it is a biological fact that Mary could not have independently furnished Jesus with her blood. What she did supply was an egg that God would use to prepare Jesus' earthly body. Mary carried in her body the egg, which contained all the chromosomes to grow the fingers, toes, hands, ears, eyes, and nose, but she did not contribute directly to His blood; that was the work of the Holy Spirit.

LUKE 1:35

35 And the angel answered and said unto her, The Holy Ghost shall come upon thee, and the power of the Highest shall overshadow thee: therefore also that holy thing which shall be born of thee shall be called the Son of God.

As a baby develops in the womb, it is separated from the mother by the placenta. The mother's blood comes to the placenta, but stops there. It bathes the outside of the placenta, then, through the process of osmosis, diffusion, and capillary attraction, the necessary nutrients and oxygen flow through the membrane that separates mother from child, and eventually pass into the baby's bloodstream through the umbilical cord. The infant's umbilical cord is attached to the placenta, not the mother. The mother's blood circulates on one side of the placenta. The baby's blood circulates on the other side of the placenta.

The baby's blood, which is a self-contained cardio-vascular system, doesn't mingle with its mother's blood. It receives nutrition and oxygen indirectly from her blood, but does not receive her blood itself. In fact, the child's blood is often a completely different blood type than the mother's.

The significance of the virgin birth means that because Jesus was truly born of a virgin, there is only one place His blood could have come from, and it wasn't of this earth! He had His heavenly Father's blood.

As we saw before, Jesus said, "...a body hast thou prepared for me."[5] Notice, He mentions the body, but He didn't say anything about the blood. God prepared a body for Jesus, but the life of that body came down from heaven. The life is in the blood, and Jesus' blood had to come from heaven. Jesus' body was exactly like yours and mine, in every way, except His blood was like Adam's blood *before* sin came into him.

Before the cross, Jesus never knew sin. Had Adam's sinful blood been flowing through Jesus' veins, then Jesus' blood would have been useless for redemption. If Adam's death-infected blood, by way of Noah and David, had been in the Messiah, then we would have been doomed.

Sin is innate. It's just there. Unregenerate man doesn't have to do anything to become a sinner. Sin is a congenital disorder on a spiritual level. David said, "Surely I was sinful at birth, sinful from the time my mother conceived me" (Ps. 51:5 NIV).

Jesus never knew sin. He was a unique man walking this earth like you and me in every respect except that He did not know sin or sickness. Jesus lived and walked as Adam should have lived and walked. Had it not been for Adam's sin, all human beings could have lived with the birthright of eternal life and goodness as sons of God.

Throughout the thousands of years spanning Genesis 2 to Acts 2, there were exactly two God-men with pure blood, Adam and Jesus. They are the First and Last Adam respectively. (1 Cor. 15:45.)

Nowhere in the Bible do we find that Jesus was ever sick with a cold or headache. Jesus was never sick until He voluntarily became a curse for us. (Matt. 8:17.)

There was such virtue in Jesus' blood that he could touch lepers and heal them. He was so filled with life that he could heal a blind man or a deaf-mute. (John 9:6; Mark 7:33-35.)

Before the fall, Adam could not have been sick as long as he had untainted, divine life in his blood. After the fall he became susceptible to sickness and death. If we were more yielded to divine life of God, we wouldn't be sick either.

Adam's blood, at first, had life in it. His blood had the ability to resist any kind of injury or infection until it became polluted with sin. As I mentioned earlier, he didn't succumb to physical death until he was nine hundred and thirty years old.

Notice that man's life expectancy diminished steadily down through the years. In Abraham's days men lived to be a hundred and twenty years old or more. By the time of the Exodus they were dying at seventy or eighty years old, and that was the result of their disobedience.[6]

From a scriptural point of view, longevity is the birthright of the believer, "With long life will I satisfy him, and shew him my salvation" (Ps. 91:16). The blood of Christ is the elixir of life. The remedy for premature death is in His blood.

I have a friend who at one time ran a blood bank in Kansas City. They prepared blood and blood byproducts for the medical industry. They delivered blood all over the country. My friend explained to me that they prepared blood that contained a special serum that had disease-resistant properties. In other words, the medicine was in the blood before the blood was sent out.

Now imagine if you received a transfusion of Jesus' blood. There is no way Jesus could have contracted a bacterial or viral infection, or any disease for that matter. His blood was charged with life. It had preventive and curative power. I am sure Jesus was exposed to sickness. Many sick people touched Him and were healed instantly. Disease could not exist in His blood.

What would happen if you had that kind of life in you? Your body would heal so quickly that you wouldn't even know you had been sick. You can have it, by faith!

I am not implying that you will never die physically. You will eventually, unless Jesus returns first. With God's power in your blood you can live a long, healthy life upon this earth before you go to heaven. You don't have to die sick. When it is your time, you can go to sleep and wake up in glory.

Jesus was free from death. No one was capable of killing Jesus. He had to surrender his life. Jesus said, "Therefore doth my Father love me, because I lay down my life, that I might take it again. No man taketh it from me, but I lay it down of myself..." (John 10:17,18). He told Pontius Pilate, "...Thou couldest have no power at all against me, except it were given thee from above" (John 19:11). On the cross He said, "...It is finished: and he bowed his head, and gave up the ghost" (John 19:30).

The Bible didn't say that Jesus died. It says He *"gave up the ghost."* Man could not have killed Jesus. There was no way humanity could have killed our Lord. He had divine life in Him. If He had not willingly given up His life; He could not have died. For Him to die, something had to happen to His blood. He had to receive the nature of death into Himself.

BLOOD, A CORRUPTIBLE SUBSTANCE

Now look at what Peter had to say about the blood of Jesus.

1 PETER 1:18,19

18 Forasmuch as ye know that ye were not redeemed with corruptible things, as silver and gold, from your vain conversation received by tradition from your fathers;

19 But with the precious blood of Christ, as of a lamb without blemish and without spot.

We were not redeemed with anything corruptible. This is important information to put into your spirit. Make it one of the fundamental tenets of your faith.

Leviticus 17:11 says, "The life of the flesh is in the blood…." The religious Jews observed strict rules against the drinking of blood. It was a dietary prohibition with deep spiritual significance.

Human blood is one of the most corruptible substances on earth. It is the ideal breeding environment for thousands of diseases.

When talking to my friend who ran the blood bank, I asked him, "If you were to take human blood and put it in an open basin, without refrigeration or preservatives, how long would it be before it started going bad?"

Without hesitation he answered, "It starts to corrupt immediately. Blood that's not handled properly can't be used in a transfusion because it would become polluted."

Blood will begin to decompose almost immediately after it is shed. Germs are attracted to it.

Again, we were not redeemed with anything corruptible. We were redeemed with the incorruptible blood of Jesus! It is important that you understand this concept.

Jesus' blood was and is incorruptible. Ordinary blood is extremely corruptible. The Jewish priests knew about the corruptible nature of blood. Imagine the odor that must have been in the tabernacle during the times of sacrifice. Frankly, our Judeo-Christian tradition is a bloody tradition and was not a pretty sight.

In the old temple there must have been the stench of countless bulls, goats, sheep, and turtledoves that were slaughtered before the altars. The priests cut the throats of the sacrificial beasts, and the blood flowed freely. Doubtless the gore attracted flies! The temple must have permeated with the putrid odor of death.

When I was a boy in Texas, I would go to the slaughterhouse where the cattle were butchered for bones for my dog. To this day I can vividly remember the sights and smells of that bloody place.

Can you imagine going to church with swarms of flies and the aroma of a slaughterhouse? I suppose our modern processing plants are much cleaner than those old temples. Those hot, sticky, bloody places must have been dreadful. Even the blood of the purest sacrificial animals was corruptible. As they slaughtered the beasts they spilled corruptible blood. Perhaps you never thought of temple worship in those terms.

You can see why the Jews had an aversion to blood. Besides the ceremonial prohibitions, they knew all too well how corruptible it was. They wouldn't eat any animal that had been strangled. The kosher way of butchering an animal was to first cut its throat, while it was yet alive, then hang it upside down and let the last drop of blood be pumped out by a beating heart. Otherwise its corrupt blood would contaminate the meat.

On a practical level, meat is cooked before it's eaten to sterilize the blood. Old-timers would "jerk" their beef to preserve it. Dehydrating the meat removes the blood, preventing spoilage. Without refrigeration, fresh meat will spoil because it contains corruptible blood. Likewise, undertakers remove the blood from dead bodies and replace it with an inert, embalming fluid, so the body won't decompose before burial. In certain places in South America, where embalming is unavailable, the law requires the dead to be buried within five hours. Otherwise the bodies will begin to decay and spawn infectious disease.

THE INCORRUPTIBLE BLOOD OF JESUS

Now you know why the Jews were horrified when Jesus stood among a crowd on the feast day and cried, "…Verily, verily, I say unto you, Except ye eat the flesh of the Son of man, and *drink his blood,* ye have no life in you" (John 6:53).

Drink his blood? Appalling! This went beyond outrage. To the Jewish mind it was ghastly and abhorrent. They accused Jesus of blasphemy and demon possession. Nothing He could have said would have offended them more deeply.

This was the end of Jesus' popularity. Before Jesus started talking about His blood, huge crowds followed Him and sought to touch Him. Now only a handful remained faithful. They didn't understand that Jesus was saying that there was divine life in His blood. He was the manna that came down from heaven, the living bread. (John 6:47-51.)

He was and is life. The absolute, divine life of God was pumping through the veins of a sin-free human being, Jesus Christ, God in the flesh. He was offering this gift of life to anyone who would believe. Their religious minds prevented them from receiving the truth.

In this we see the significance of the bread and the wine, and the flesh and the blood, of our Christian sacrament. Now we can begin to grasp the power of Peter's sermon delivered immediately after Pentecost. Remember, this was the very first sermon delivered by anyone after the resurrection. His text was aimed at the Jews, and it was a familiar messianic psalm:

ACTS 2:26,27

26 Therefore did my heart rejoice, and my tongue was glad; moreover also my *flesh* shall rest in hope:

27 Because thou wilt not leave my soul in hell, neither wilt thou suffer thine Holy One to see *corruption.*

No corruption of the Messiah's flesh spoke volumes to the Jews. Three thousand Jews were immediately saved upon hearing this. (Acts 2:41.)

Likewise, in Acts 13:35 Paul preached to the Jews at Antioch, with the same argument, saying, "Wherefore he saith also in another psalm, Thou shalt not suffer thine Holy One" [Christ] "to see corruption." *The Amplified Bible* calls it, "putrefaction and dissolution of the grave."

God would not allow His Holy One to undergo the *putrefaction* or *dissolution* of the grave. That is the most convincing argument that Jesus was the Messiah. He did not have corruptible, Adamic blood. After Jesus' death, His body didn't decompose!

Contrast that to Lazarus. His flesh was severely decomposed by the fourth day after his death. He didn't have heaven's blood. Jesus said to His disciples, "...Our friend Lazarus sleepeth...," meaning that he was dead (John 11:11). When He later came to the home of Mary and Martha, the sisters of Lazarus, "...he found that he had lain in the grave four days already" (v. 17). When Jesus went to Lazarus' tomb and ordered that the stone be taken away, Martha said to Him, "...Lord, by this time he stinketh: for he hath been dead four days" (v. 39).

The normal putrefaction and dissolution of the grave had already begun. That is what happens to flesh when it is not embalmed. Embalming slows the process of putrefaction.

For three days Jesus' body lay on a slab of stone in the hot land of Israel. It was a land with livestock in the streets, a place infested with flies and disease, yet His body didn't swell and His flesh didn't smell.

After His conquest of death and hell, Jesus came to take up His body again, and it was better than when He left it. Mary came to His tomb expecting to find a battered, bruised corpse. However, He was very much alive and physically sound. This is irrefutable proof that Jesus had no sin or death in His blood.

GOD'S LIFE SPILLED OUT

Jesus came to this earth as our lifeline from heaven. The culture of divine-life was inside His body. In order to release heaven's life, He had to submit His back to the brutal scourge of jagged pieces of bone and metal woven into each strand of the whip. Nevertheless, He *willingly* allowed His back to be raked open so healing would flow toward us.

Jesus had ample power to resist His tormentors. He could have spoken with a whisper and struck dead the man who was flogging Him, but He didn't. With every cruel blow, His blood spewed into the atmosphere. Thus, eternal life was transported to the earth, encapsulated in the vessel of Jesus' body, like a vial of smelling salts which, when broken, pours out into the air.

When I was a boy on that Texas ranch, we would mark the lambs by cutting notches in their ears. Fine streams of blood would spray into the air from those tiny severed vessels. I have been baptized with warm, sticky lamb's blood. By the end of each workday it was in my face, my hair, and even in my mouth. I know about showers of blood.

The blood of the Lamb of God was showered upon a human race, desperate to be saved. His heart was racing, probably at a rate of 200 beats per minute, or more. He spent over six hours with His back flayed open while His throbbing heart pumped His precious life out of Him.[7]

Life-giving blood ran over His earthly body with each beat. It sprayed into the atmosphere of this planet and dripped into the dust of the earth. Since Calvary, eternal life has been within the reach of every man.

God formed the original Adam from the dust of the ground and breathed life into him, but that life was lost. Now, through the Second Adam, that same life is back in this earth.

Some of the actual blood must still be here because it's eternal! Certainly it wasn't destroyed. Perhaps it somehow dispersed throughout the planet, into the atmosphere, into the dust, and into the water. The rest, as we shall see, covered Him in hell, and the remainder He carried with Him into heaven when He ascended.

The life of God is an actual, eternal, heavenly substance. It is not an idea or a philosophical concept. It is the very real, *tangible* life of God that Jesus Christ, the Second Adam, had pumping through His veins. Along with the red cells, white cells, and other *natural* compounds in His blood, there was an invisible, cleansing, life-giving substance, which flowed through Him from the throne of God. "And he shewed me a pure river of water of life, *clear as crystal,* proceeding out of the throne of God and of the Lamb" (Rev. 22:1).

That river of life was channeled into this world through the heart and veins of Jesus Christ. It is yet available to all those who believe on the name of Jesus Christ and who receive Him as Lord.

You can receive that life into you. It is as simple as breathing in God, breathing out praise. Jesus is life. He let His life seep from Him so that it could be transfused into you and me. It's eternal, and it's here right now for all who believe in their hearts and confess with their mouths. (Rom. 10:9,10.)

First Peter 2:24 works because those many wounds on the body of Jesus were the channels, the small fountains, of eternal life that God opened for us. Healing came from heaven through Jesus' torn flesh.

Likewise, we have access into heaven through His flesh.

HEBREWS 10:19,20

19 Having therefore, brethren, boldness to enter into the holiest by the blood of Jesus,

20 By a new and living way, which he hath consecrated for us, through the veil, that is to say, his flesh.

Figuratively, to reach God, we pass through Jesus' wounded side, being covered with His blood, just as an infant passes through the womb. When we are born again, we are baptized in Jesus' blood. More precisely, unless we are covered with His blood, we can't be born again.[8]

First Peter 2:24 doesn't work just because Jesus was wounded. Don't fixate on the wounds. It is what comes through those wounds that give life. The thieves on the cross were wounded. Many people have been wounded. I have a large scar on my side from a wound I received as a teenager. But divine life didn't pump out of me when my flesh was opened.

There is only one spring of eternal life: Jesus the Lamb of God.

CHAPTER 3

Light and Life

Have you ever heard anyone say, "I plead the blood of Jesus"? There's a profound truth here that some have forgotten. The old-timers used to plead the blood as a part of their daily lives. In this chapter we will shine God's light on the significance of pleading the blood.

We have just learned that the blood of Jesus gives us eternal life, brings us into vital union with Christ,[1] and heals us.[2] Now we shall learn why demons are terrified of the blood of Jesus.

In the last days God is raising up an army. Over that army is a blood-stained banner that represents the absolute victory that Jesus won over the adversary. His victory is our victory.

God raising Jesus from the dead and the blood He used to raise Him are the heart and the heartbeat of the gospel. We cannot allow anyone to negate the importance of the blood in our lives.

In the past, most Christians blindly followed their church creeds and traditions. Whatever the denomination believed, and whatever their pastors preached, is what Christians believed. Today, I hope, we are more scholarly. We should want to know for ourselves what the Word of God says. It is all right to question traditions. Jesus said, "...seek, and ye shall find" (Matt. 7:7). After all, it is the truth we *know* that sets us free.[3]

It is *nobler* to search the Scriptures than to mindlessly follow religious tradition. We should strive to know not only what we believe, but also why we believe it. Some things bear repeating to see another facet of the blood.

We learned from Leviticus 17:11, the life of all flesh is in the blood. In Genesis 2:7 we saw that God formed Adam from the dust, or elemental particles, of the ground. Adam then had a body, but it was not yet a living body—there was still no life in it.

I have seen beautiful marble sculptures that were so lifelike it seemed they should breathe and move. They were exquisite in form and shape, but there was no life in them. They were without the ability to live, breathe, or think. They were just forms.

God formed man from the dust of the earth, or from the elements of the earth. When I was in grade school, my physical science teacher once said that the mineral content of common, garden soil was proportionately the same as the mineral content of the human body. That seems plausible.

Some small children eat dirt. Today many people yearn to return to a simple life, back to earth, so to speak. That is understandable. There is something in us that draws us to our origins. We are drawn to the genesis of man.

God breathed into man the breath of life, and life is in the blood; therefore, there is a very close relationship between our nostrils and our bloodstream. The air we breathe in contains oxygen, which goes directly into our blood. Likewise, the air we exhale contains waste gasses, which come out of our blood. In goes the good; out goes the bad. With every breath, our blood is charged with oxygen.

Without oxygen, there could be no biological life in man. As we discussed earlier, Adam's first breath came directly from God. It went straight into his nostrils, inflated his lungs, and charged his blood with the very life and nature of God. When God's life began pumping through Adam's veins, that lifeless statue called Adam came alive.

Can you picture the moment when Adam first opened his eyes and looked at his Father? What a moment! He gazed at his Father. His Father gazed back at him. They were vitally connected. The same life was in their blood. Adam was a living soul, alive with the very life and nature of God. He was truly a son of God.

THE LIGHT OF THE WORLD

Now let's delve into pleading the blood. The blood of Jesus is luminous!

JOHN 1:1-5,9

1 In the beginning was the Word, and the Word was with God, and the Word was God.

2 The same was in the beginning with God.

3 All things were made by him; and without him was not any thing made that was made.

4 In him was life; and *the life was the light* of men.

5 And the light shineth in darkness; and the darkness comprehended it not...

9 That was the true Light, which lighteth every man that cometh into the world.

Notice, God's life is *light.* I call it luminous life. James refers to God as "the Father of lights, with whom is no variableness, neither shadow of turning" (James 1:17). God is the Father of light. God's breath of life went into Adam's blood and lit him up.

Adam received the spark of life. He could now correspond with his environment. "That was the true Light, which lighteth every man that cometh into the world" (v. 9).

There are two kinds of life: divine life and *biological life.* Biological life is like a little fire inside each person.

Biological energy depends on a form of controlled, internal combustion called metabolism. Oxygen and food, our fuel, are converted into heat and energy. All people have within them a spark of biological life. Biological life began when God created Adam and continues today. Every organic creature has biological life.

There is another kind of life called spiritual life. Paul was referring to this in his epistle to the Roman Christians, "For the law of the Spirit of life in Christ Jesus hath made me free from the law of sin and death" (Rom. 8:2).

I could say it like this: The spiritual life that was in Jesus now makes me free from the spiritual death, which came through Adam as the result of sin.[4]

JOHN 1:4,5

4   In him was life; and the life was the light of men.

5   And the light shineth in darkness; and the darkness *comprehended* it not.

You could replace the word *comprehend* with the words *apprehend*[5] or *arrest*. The darkness apprehended it not. Darkness could not arrest it.

Light, natural or spiritual, always overpowers darkness. In a photographer's darkroom the doors are sealed, the walls are painted with light-absorbing pigments, and everything is pitch black. You can strike one little match, and the darkness will be penetrated!

The vast darkness of outer space cannot overpower the light of a single, distant star. Distance can't stop it. Darkness can't arrest it. Light *always* overpowers darkness.

In west Texas you can see for great distances. On clear nights, near the Big Bend National Park, you can actually see out for two hundred and fifty miles. From a mountaintop at night, you can spot one tiny light miles across the valley—someone's little porch light. All that darkness doesn't even slow the light down.

Natural light is marvelous, but spiritual light far exceeds natural light in every way.

JOHN 1:6-9

6   There was a man sent from God, whose name was John.

7   The same came for a witness, to bear witness of the Light, that all men through him might believe.

8   He was not that Light, but was sent to bear witness of that Light.

9   That was the true Light, which lighteth every man that cometh into the world.

In Genesis 1:3 we read these words: "And God said, Let there be light: and there was light." The Hebrew word for "light" is *owr* (pronounced "ore").[6] This word is used, not only literally to refer to luminance, but also figuratively, to indicate everything that is good, happy, filled with joy, or wholesome. In other words, everything that God is, His light is. God is light. (1 John 1:5.) Now let's read from Genesis again:

GENESIS 1:1-3

1   In the beginning God created the heaven and the earth.

2   And the earth was without form, and void; and darkness was upon the face of the deep. And the Spirit of God moved upon the face of the waters.

3   And God said, Let there be light: and there was light.

God said, "Let there be light," and suddenly the whole universe erupted into being: The stars began to shine, the heavens reverberated with joy, and goodness became visible. Then He said, *"It was good."* He said, "Let there be light:" [Let this universe be filled with goodness! Let this universe be filled with power! Let this universe be filled with joy!], "and there was light." The darkness of the void gave way to light and joy. Light completely overpowered the darkness.

God created "the greater light" [the sun—natural light] "to rule the day, and the lesser light" [the moon—natural light] "to rule the night: he made the stars also" (v. 16).

We must consider the so-called prince of darkness whom God had banished from heaven. Satan fancies himself the prince of spiritual darkness. His dwelling place is in the dark regions because he is darkness. Stereotypically, the bad guys wear black hats.

Satan is the prince of darkness, but God is the Father of lights.

JOHN 1:4

4   In him was life; and the life was the light of men.

JOHN 3:16,17

16 For God so loved the world, that he gave his only begotten
Son, that whosoever believeth in him should not perish, but
have everlasting life.

17 For God sent not his Son into the world to condemn the
world; but that the world through him might be saved.

THE ENTRANCE OF LIGHT

Jesus is called the Light of the world. Jesus, the Word
made Flesh, said, "I am the light of the world" (John
8:12). The psalmist said, "The entrance of thy words
giveth light" (Ps. 119:130).

Light is life, and Jesus is the Word of God. He is the
very Light that *shineth in darkness, and the darkness apprehended it not.* He is the Light that darkness couldn't stop.
He is the Light that even the darkness of sin could not
hold back.

Contrary to what Satan may have believed, he could
have never overcome Jesus. Darkness cannot overpower
light. Had Jesus not laid down His life voluntarily, Satan
would have never gotten to first base. If Satan had known
who the Lord of glory was, he would not have crucified
Him. (See 1 Cor. 2:8.) By doing so, Satan fell right in line
with God's secret plan for the conquest of hell.

JOHN 3:17-21

17 For God sent not his Son into the world to condemn the
world; but that the world through him might be saved.

18 He that believeth on him is not condemned: but he that believeth not is condemned already, because he hath not believed in the name of the only begotten son of God.

19 And this is the condemnation, that light is come into the world, and men loved darkness rather than light, because their deeds were evil.

20 For every one that doeth evil *hateth the light, neither cometh to the light,* lest his deeds should be reproved.

21 But he that doeth truth cometh to the light, that his deeds may be made manifest, that they are wrought in God.

Those who love light are drawn to the Light. Those who are evil in thoughts or deeds avoid God's Light. Most murders, burglaries, muggings, and rapes occur at night because evil people feel more comfortable under the cloak of darkness.

Good people feel comfortable walking around in broad daylight with their deeds and actions open to God and everybody. I don't have to sneak around because I have nothing to hide. It is a wonderful feeling just to be able to walk around in front of God and everyone with no sense of shame.

THE LIGHT REVEALED

God prepared an earth-body for Jesus through Mary, a virgin espoused to Joseph. It was through the miracle of the anointing of the Holy Spirit that God fathered Jesus. The child growing within her was a "holy thing" (Luke

1:35), *whose* holy blood came from His heavenly Father. In Christ's blood was pure, divine life: "In him was life; and the life was the light of men" (John 1:4). Jesus' blood was full of life and glory. If it had God's *life* in it, then it had to have God's *light* in it. We see visible light around us every day. But there are invisible wavelengths of light as well. There are infrared and ultraviolet wavelengths of light, which are not visible to the human eye. For the most part, God's kingdom is invisible to the natural eye. (Col. 1:15.) It is beyond the spectrum of human vision, but it is there. That light is known and seen in the spirit world. Evil men hate that light.

God's light torments demons. Devils cried out in pain in the presence of Jesus, "Thou Jesus of Nazareth.... I know thee who thou art; the Holy One of God" (Luke 4:34). Jesus radiated blinding, brilliant, spiritual light. They knew who He was. Every born-again believer is filled with that same spiritual light. We can torment devils!

On more than one occasion I have had demoniacs say to me, *"I know who you are."* One demon-possessed man hissed at me, "Larry Huggins, I know who you are."

I answered, "I know you do! Shut up." That man didn't know my name, but the demon within him did.

Jesus is the Light of the world. As he walked upon this earth He had a light *within* and about Him. He radiated spiritual light.

Chemical flashlights are popular emergency lights, especially among motorists and boating enthusiasts. No batteries are needed to activate them. You just twist the tube; two liquids run together generating liquid luminance. Liquid-light glows beautifully. Figuratively, Jesus had liquid-light in His veins. Jesus took Peter, James, and John up the mountain where "He was transfigured before them; and His face shone like the sun..." (Matt. 17:2 NIV). This scripture tells us that *His skin shone as brightly as the sun.* Jesus had light in Him, and apparently He could control it. He seemingly turned it on or off at will, revealing Himself to whomever He would.

Paul saw Jesus on the road to Damascus, and a light was shining from Him. It was brighter than the noonday sun, and inside that light was Jesus Christ, saying, "...Saul, why do you persecute me?" (Acts 22:7 NIV). Wherever Jesus is there is light, because He is the Light of the world.

THE POWER OF LIGHT

Psalm 27:1 says, "The LORD is my light and my salvation; whom shall I fear?..." Evil flees from light. "...Resist the devil, and he will flee from you" (James 4:7).

For example, I have never understood why people are afraid of snakes. Man has dominion over snakes. The snakes are the ones who are afraid! They flee from people. Likewise, demons flee in terror from a child of God.

Through our union with Jesus Christ we have become light, and we have nothing to fear! Psalm 27:1 says, "The Lord is my light and my salvation; whom shall I fear?"

The Son of God is brighter than the noonday sun in all its brilliance. "The LORD God is a sun and shield..." (Ps. 84:11).

Light can be both a weapon and a defense. The United States Department of Defense has laser weapons. Lasers are high intensity, coherent light. We have something more powerful—the light of God, the sword of the Spirit.

One of the brightest lights that man has been able to develop is called a calcium arc light. It is so bright it cannot be viewed with the naked eye. It would be blinding. Yet, when viewed against the sun, a calcium arc light would look like a dark spot because the sun is so much brighter.

Our Savior is brighter than the noonday sun! I can hardly imagine that kind of brightness. Romans 13:12 tells us, "The night is far spent, the day is at hand: let us therefore cast off the works of darkness, and let us put on the armour of light."

We always talk about the weapons of our warfare, about the armor of God and the helmet of salvation. (Eph. 6:13-17.) The scriptures tell us, "The weapons we fight with are not the weapons of the world. On the contrary, they have divine power to demolish strongholds" (2 Cor. 10:4 NIV). The helmet of salvation is not like a Roman legionnaire's helmet made of iron or bronze. It is a helmet of pure divine-light. All the armor of God is light.

We wear the breastplate of righteousness. It is pure light. Adam didn't have any clothing. He didn't need mere earthly garments; he had the life of God in his blood, breathed into him by the Father of light, illuminating him! He walked with God, and God is Light.

Our loins are girt about with truth.[7] Truth is light. "The entrance of thy words giveth light..." (Ps. 119:130). Our feet are shod with the preparation of the gospel of peace,[8] which again is light!

We are children of light. We are instructed to walk in the light. Ephesians 5:8 says, "For ye were sometimes darkness, but now are ye light in the Lord...." You are light! Say this to yourself, "I am light! I used to walk in darkness, but now I am light!"

Notice it doesn't say that you *just* walk in the light; it says you *are* the light! Oh, if we could only see ourselves as God sees us! We are luminous!

Late one stormy night I stopped along a dark, secluded stretch of road, on the outskirts of town, to pick up a hitchhiker. He was wet and dirty, but more than that, there was an evil presence about him. Ordinarily, I do not stop for hitchhikers, but I was impressed by the Holy Spirit to help him. When he got into the car, it was as if the devil himself had climbed in.

I casually asked the stranger how he was doing. He literally growled, "How am I doing? I'll tell you how I'm doing. I ain't doing good at all! I'm an addict. I just got out of jail. Those cops didn't give me no medication, and I had to lick heroine 'cold turkey.' I was sick the whole time. My so-called friends had me busted. I owe my lawyer a thousand dollars, and he tells me the cops have another warrant out on me. I'll tell you how I'm doing. I ain't doing good at all. I'm doing bad! I want some dope, and I'm looking to kill the person who had me busted!"

The lightning flashed through the window, and his face looked monstrous. He was scowling at me with a homicidal gleam in his eyes. He was panting; his nose was flaring and his chest heaving. He could barely contain his rage.

I swallowed the lump in my throat and bravely said, "I know Someone who can help you. Take my hand and pray with me."

Desperately, the hitchhiker seized upon that bit of hope. "I need someone to help me before I do something terrible!"

As I led him in the sinner's prayer, he gripped my hand hard and began to shake and cry. He begged God for mercy, "Oh, please help me, God. I promise I'll try and do right. Please, God, please…"

I interrupted, "Don't make promises. Just love Him."

He got it! "Oh, Jesus," he said, "I love You so much! Thank You, Lord, for saving me…."

As that man prayed, he was gloriously saved. His skin began to shine with a heavenly glimmer. It became so bright you could have read a Bible by it. That hitchhiker was filled with the light and life of God. He was literally translated out of the kingdom of darkness into the Kingdom of Light, right before my eyes!

I will never forget his hair, beard, and eyes. He looked like Jesus. One instant he was a wretch, and the next, a son of God, bathed with a heavenly glow.

Later he said, "You know, a few minutes ago I was so full of hate, I wanted to kill someone. Now I don't want to kill anyone—I love everyone."

THE LIFE OF THE WORLD

In John 8:12 Jesus said, "...I am the light of the world: he that followeth me shall not walk in darkness, but shall have the light of life."

To me this is not just speaking of light, but also of the blood of Jesus.

Jesus said that anyone who followed Him would have the light of life. He had the light of life, and that life was in His veins because the life of all flesh is in the blood. Jesus' life was in His blood so His light was in His blood also. In Jesus' case, blood and light go together, just as blood and life go together.

1 JOHN 1:5-7

5　This then is the message which we have heard of him, and declare unto you, that God is light, and in him is no darkness at all [God transmitted His life-light into Adam].

6   If we say that we have fellowship with him, and walk in darkness, we lie, and do not the truth:

7   But if we *walk in the light, as he is in the light,* we have fellowship one with another, and the blood of Jesus Christ his Son cleanseth us from all sin.

When I talk about the blood of Jesus, I am talking about the inseparable qualities of divine light and divine life.

If we walk in the *light,* as He is in the *light,* we have fellowship one with another, and the *blood* of Jesus Christ His Son cleanseth us from all sin. Read it this way: If we walk in the Word, in which is truth, His blood cleanses us....

The truth and Word of God pumped through Jesus' veins. It was life and light! God can get so much into one thing. The blood of Jesus covers it all.

COLOSSIANS 1:12-14

12 Giving thanks unto the Father, which hath made us meet [able] to be partakers of the inheritance of the saints in light:

13 Who hath delivered us from the power of darkness, and hath translated us into the kingdom of his dear *Son:*

14 In whom we have redemption through his blood, even the forgiveness of sins.

The word "redemption" can also be translated "deliverance."[9] In whom we have deliverance—deliverance from darkness, sin, and the devil! The Knox translation says it this way: "In the Son of God, in his blood, we find the redemption that sets us free from our sins."[10]

We were translated out of the kingdom of darkness into the kingdom of God's dear Son through the blood of Jesus Christ. (Col. 1:13,14.) We were moved out of darkness into light by the blood because divine light *is* in the blood of Jesus.

COLOSSIANS 1:15,16

15 Who is the image of the invisible God, the firstborn of every creature:

16 For by him were all things created, that are in heaven, and that are in earth, visible and invisible, whether they be thrones, or dominions, or principalities, or powers: all things were created by him, and for him.

The Bible says that Lucifer was created to be the high, anointed cherub, to lead in music and worship before Almighty God in heaven. He was perfect and full of wisdom until iniquity was found in him. (See Ezek. 28:12-15.) God didn't make him evil. He did that to himself. It was after Lucifer sinned that he became darkness.

The angelic host, who joined Lucifer in treason, was also created by and for God. They too were banished forever from heaven because they rebelled against God. There are scriptures suggesting demons are fallen angels.[11]

The prince of the power of the air and his cohorts were driven from heaven and fled to inhabit the dark, lower regions of this world. (See Eph. 2:2.)

For the most part, they carry out their evil pursuits through witting and unwitting human beings, under the cloak of deception.

COLOSSIANS 1:17-20

17 And He [Jesus] is before all things, and by him all things consist.

18 And he is the head of the body, the church: who is the beginning, the firstborn from the dead; that in all things he might have the preeminence.

19 For it pleased the Father that in him should all fulness dwell;

20 And, having made peace through the blood of his cross, by him to reconcile all things unto himself; by him, I say, whether they be things in earth, or things in heaven.

Inside Jesus was the fullness of God. God is light. Inside Jesus' body was life and light. Now He has become our Light.

COLOSSIANS 2:10,11

10 And ye are complete in him, which is the head of all *principality and power*:

11 In whom also ye are circumcised with the circumcision made without hands, in putting off the body of the sins of the flesh by the circumcision of Christ.

If we, as children of God, continue in sin, we dim the light that is inside us. Our light becomes obscured because our deeds are evil. To remain bright, we must "...walk in the light, as he is in the light" (1 John 1:7).

CHAPTER 4

You Are in the Light

COLOSSIANS 2:12-15

12 Buried with him in baptism, wherein also ye are risen with him through the faith of the operation of God, who hath raised him from the dead.

13 And you, being dead in your sins and the uncircumcision of your flesh, hath he quickened together with him, having forgiven you all trespasses;

14 Blotting out the handwriting of ordinances that was against us, which was contrary to us, and took it out of the way, nailing it to his cross;

15 And having spoiled principalities and powers, he made a shew of them openly, triumphing over them in it.

This is an astonishing story, but one of the least understood by the body of Christ. Most Christians don't understand exactly what happened immediately before, during, and after the crucifixion of Jesus Christ. John tells us, "For this purpose the Son of God was manifested, that he might destroy the works of the devil" (1 John 3:8).

Jesus' mission on earth was to destroy the works of the devil. He came from heaven and entered a body prepared for Him. All of God's power was squeezed into that body. He was more than a match for the powers of darkness. Nevertheless, Satan spun a wicked web of deceit, lying in wait to snare Jesus.

The devil put it in Judas' heart to betray innocent blood. Jesus was arrested in the garden by temple guards who turned Him over to the Jewish priests who had conspired to sentence Him to death. It was a sentence that would be carried out by the Romans who occupied Jerusalem.

Later, agitated mobs would cry unto the Roman ruler, Pilot, *"His blood be upon us, and our children"* (Matt. 27:25). They didn't know what they were saying. Jesus submitted to crucifixion. It would have been impossible for them to do the things they did to Him had God not allowed it. (See Acts 2:23.)

At the time of crucifixion, manifested spiritual darkness surrounded the earth. Although the sun came up that grim morning, it was deathly dark because of the concentration of evil around the hill called "Golgotha," "the place of a skull" (Mark 15:22).

Jesus had come into this dark earth as the perfect Lamb of God, without spot or blemish with heaven's light in His blood, to defeat evil. He was the Light of the world, but that light that was inside Him had to go into the world. Thus, He allowed Himself to be taken and beaten, His back laid open until the blood ran down. He permitted Himself to hang naked and abandoned upon the cruel cross of Calvary.

2 CORINTHIANS 5:21

21 For he hath made him to be sin for us, who knew no sin; that we might be made the righteousness of God in him.

For a moment God Himself turned His back on our substitute in sin. It must have been a difficult thing to do, but this was God's master plan.

LIGHT POURED OUT

Golgotha was swallowed in gross darkness, but soon a light would shine unto all mankind, forever, inextinguishable. "...And the darkness comprehended it not" (John 1:5).

Perhaps, during the crucifixion of Christ, Jerusalem became dark with devils! I presume they may have come from every region of earth to mock the Son of God. I can visualize hordes of wicked demons celebrating in hellish jubilee. They celebrated what they thought was the victory of the prince of darkness over the Son of God. They mocked Him, laughing, teasing, taunting, deriding, and jeering in discordant shrieks—a chorus of the damned, "Ha, ha, we've got Him now! We've got Him now! We've got God's little Lamb." They cursed Him shamelessly, "The Son of God is doomed. Mankind is too. Look! Look! We've got Him now!"

At the end of the physical ordeal, Jesus said, "…It is finished: and he bowed his head, and gave up the ghost" (John 19:30). Now real suffering commenced. Under the crushing weight of sin, His soul began sinking into the lowest depths of hell. Some people will not accept the fact that Jesus went to hell, but the psalmist wrote, "For thou wilt not leave my soul in hell" (Ps. 16:10). Peter quoted this prophetic psalm in his Pentecost sermon, and Paul preached it at Antioch. (Acts 2:25-27,30; 13:35.)

If He didn't pay the price, who will? If He didn't descend into the deepest depths, how could He ascend to the heights and fill all things? David said, "If I ascend up into heaven, thou art there: if I make my bed in hell, behold, thou art there" (Ps. 139:8).

Jesus Himself said, "For as Jonas was three days and three nights in the whale's belly; so shall the Son of man be three days and three nights in the heart of the earth" (Matt. 12:40).

I imagine a shadowy swarm of satanic spirits, swirling and swooping around the paralyzed Son of God as they descended into the dungeon of the damned. There, in the foreboding gloom of hell, they continued their insane celebration: whirling as dervishes, seized with frenzy, leaping about, screeching and howling, drunken with demon pride. Emboldened by Jesus' apparent helplessness, they spewed vileness upon Him and raked Him with demon claws.

POWER OVER DARKNESS

Once, it seemed, I was visited by every demon in Hyderabad, India. As I lay awake, alone on my bed, the night before a crusade, a parade of demons passed through my room. I saw them as clearly as you are seeing the words on this book. They came though the wall. Each one was more hideous than the next. They were similar in appearance to the pagan idols and tribal masks you may have seen, but more grotesque. Each foul spirit would approach me in turn, coming extremely close to my face, glaring at me with their unimaginably evil eyes, then passing out of sight through the wall behind my head, only to be replaced by a creature even more bizarre.

I suppose the word had gotten out among the demon population of India: A man of God is here—let's pay him a visit.

Obviously this spectacle was meant to intimidate me before my crusade or dissuade me from preaching. I was unmoved. In fact, I found it curiously entertaining. After about an hour of this absurdity, I rose up and said quietly and calmly, "Okay, now you've seen me, and I've seen you, and I'm here to do the works of God—I plead the blood of Jesus—now be gone." Then I just lay back down and went to sleep, peacefully.

What had I to fear from this motley gang of losers? Jesus had conquered Satan, along with these sorry minions, two thousand years ago. Oh, what a wonderful crusade we had that week! The Word of God prevailed. There were miracles, signs, and wonders, and thousands of souls were set free.

We are yet celebrating the victory that Jesus won for us at Calvary. We don't have to fear demons. To their surprise, Jesus utterly defeated them from within hell itself.

All of the inhabitants of hell surrounded Jesus. For a time He seemed disarmed and defenseless. But God held the trump card. Things were going as planned. Hell's celebration was premature.

HEBREWS 2:14

14 Forasmuch then as the children are partakers of flesh and blood, he also himself likewise took part of the same; that through death he might destroy him that had the power of death, that is, the devil.

FOREVER VICTORIOUS

What the demons didn't realize is that Jesus, the Scapegoat, was yet covered in His own heavenly blood. Remember, eternal life is resident in the blood of the Lamb. The operative word here is "eternal." Because it is eternal, then it could not have been destroyed. It transcended death and hell. Yes, definitely! The spiritual essence of His blood was still upon Him.

Think back to Calvary. As long as Jesus had heaven's blood *inside* Him, He could not become sin. But when it was pumped out of Him, only then could he receive sin and death. (See 2 Cor. 5:21.) Jesus would never have been able to die, spiritually or physically, if His blood had remained in Him. There was just too much life in it for that to happen.

Psalm 22:14 says, "I am poured out like water...." His heart broke and His blood poured out. Only after His life poured out did sin come in. The plan was for Jesus to become sin so that He could gain entry into hell.

To the demons, it truly appeared that God had lost the war as Christ suffered the terrors of hell. Satan thought that he had won. What he didn't understand is that the soul of the Son of God was covered with His own spiritual blood!

For three earth-days Jesus experienced the unimaginable.

The combined sufferings of every person who had ever lived, or who would ever live upon the earth, were laid upon Him. It was all the sin of the world at once.

ISAIAH 53:10,11

10 Yet it pleased the LORD to bruise him; he hath put him to grief: when thou shalt make his soul an offering for sin....

11 He shall see of the travail of his soul, and shall be satisfied: by his knowledge shall my righteous servant justify many; for he shall bear their iniquities.

When His sufferings equaled the combined punishment of everyone, everywhere, the scales of justice were balanced. His pain matched our punishment. The penalty of sin had been paid in the coin of His sufferings.

The prophet Isaiah foretold this event, "He shall see of the travail of his soul, and shall be satisfied: by his knowledge shall my righteous servant justify many; for he shall bear their iniquities" (Isa. 53:11).

At the precise moment of equity something began to happen. A light sprang out of darkness. Can you imagine what happened in that dark underworld when the life of God, that divine substance with which Jesus had been covered, began to shine brighter and brighter? In hell a light shinned in darkness.

Jesus was transfigured in hell! He was raised into newness of life by the virtue of His own blood. Romans 6:4 says, "...Christ was raised up from the dead by the glory of the Father...." That glory was resident in His blood. The same glory of the Father, the same life in the blood that saves us, saved Jesus from death to life. It worked for Him. Where the blood of Jesus is concerned, there is not a devil in hell that can keep anyone from being saved.

Jesus needed saving. He had allowed Himself to become sin, and sin separates man from the Father. He died spiritually, or that is to say, He took upon Himself the very nature of death. He had to be reborn into the newness of life.

People have trouble with the concept of Jesus dying spiritually. Death is not the cessation of being. Death is a spiritual nature. Jesus was born again, or what the writer of Hebrews called, "...brought again from the dead."

HEBREWS 13:20

20 Now the God of peace, that *brought again from the dead our Lord Jesus,* that great shepherd of the sheep, *through the blood* of the everlasting covenant.

In the darkness He began to shine, perhaps faintly at first, but then brightly, very brightly as upon the mount of transfiguration, but in hell. The livid, luminous blood of Jesus burst forth as a supernova of demon-scorching glory!

Can you imagine the confusion and panic this caused in hell? Remember that demons avoid the light because their deeds are evil. God's light torments them. His radiant holiness causes them unbearable pain. Satan was utterly unprepared for this. There, in the citadel of the damned, God's blinding light was blazing from the luminous blood of Jesus. There was no place for demons to run. They backed away but couldn't escape. They were trapped in hell!

What was happening? This Jesus, who once seemed helpless, was now shining with unbridled power. His brilliant light burst forth from hell and instantly filled the entire universe. Rocks and mountains were transparent to His glory. There was nowhere for demons to hide.

All Jesus had to do was simply walk over to the cringing, crawling, fainting, fawning, falling, whimpering, totally defenseless devil, and stoop down and pick up the keys of death and hell. We can imagine that at this time Jesus took the keys of death and of hell.

DARKNESS DEFEATED

I can almost hear our Glorious Champion saying calmly, "These are mine. I'll use them to open the prison doors and set the captives free."[1] It was no contest!

COLOSSIANS 2:15

15 And having spoiled principalities and powers, he made a shew of them openly, *triumphing* over them in it.

The Amplified Bible says it this way: "[God] disarmed the principalities and powers that were ranged against us and made a bold display and public example of them, in triumphing over them in Him and in it [the cross]."

When I was a boy we sang about this in the Baptist church.

Up from the grave He arose,
With a mighty triumph o'er His foes.
He arose the Victor from the dark domain,
And He lives forever with His saints to reign![2]

Satan was not simply defeated by the blood of Jesus. He was publicly humiliated. God, through His prophet, accurately foretold Satan's disgraceful defeat.

ISAIAH 14:9-16

9 Hell from beneath is moved for thee to meet thee at thy coming: it stirreth up the dead for thee, even all the chief

ones of the earth; it hath raised up from their thrones all the kings of the nations.

10 All they shall speak and say unto thee, Art thou also become weak as we? art thou become like unto us?

11 Thy pomp is brought down to the grave, and the noise of thy viols: the worm is spread under thee, and the worms cover thee.

12 How art thou fallen from heaven, O Lucifer, son of the morning! how art thou cut down to the ground, which didst weaken the nations!

13 For thou hast said in thine heart, I will ascend into heaven, I will exalt my throne above the stars of God: I will sit also upon the mount of the congregation, in the sides of the north:

14 I will ascend above the heights of the clouds; I will be like the most High.

15 Yet thou shalt be brought down to hell, to the sides of the pit.

16 They that see thee shall narrowly look upon thee, and consider thee, saying, Is this the man that made the earth to tremble, that did shake kingdoms?

Later, from the isle of Patmos, John the Revelator saw the victorious and resurrected Jesus, and He doesn't look like the pictures hanging on the church walls. John describes how he heard a voice behind him that sounded like "many waters" (Rev. 1:15): "...I am Alpha and Omega, the first and the last...." "I am he that liveth, and was dead; and, behold, I am alive for evermore, Amen; and have the keys of hell and of death" (Rev. 1:11,18).

He saw the One who had been to hell and back, who outshines the noonday sun. He saw Jesus' hair, white as wool. He saw His eyes—eyes like a flame of fire. He saw His mouth—out came a two-edged sword. He saw His feet, like brass that has been burned in an oven. (vv. 14-16.)

Brass becomes incandescent at extreme temperatures. Picture Jesus' every footstep exploding like phosphorescent bombs.

Now that's my Jesus! By His blood He defeated the devil, and by His blood He has delivered us from the powers of darkness and translated us into the kingdom of His dear Son. (Col. 1:13.)

This is the true and accurate picture of the resurrected Jesus. The One who conquered death, hell, and the grave is the One who terrifies demons with blazing eyes, a sword in His mouth, and seven stars in His right hand. This is the Jesus I serve.

Revelation 7:14 (NIV) says, "...These are they who have come out of the great tribulation; they have washed their robes and made them white in the blood of the Lamb." Now can you understand how His blood can wash their robes white? They are bleached white by the intense light of His blood.

Revelation 12:10-11 says that we overcome the accuser by the blood of the Lamb and the word of our testimony. Blood and light! The saber of light comes out of our mouths now, as we speak His Word.

LIGHT RESTORED

We were made warriors of light by His blood. We are recreated in His glorious image! Begin to see yourself as He sees you.

By virtue of the new birth, I am convinced that the light and life of His blood are *in* us as well as *upon* us.[3] It is a new-creation fact that His Word is in us, and it comes forth from us as a two–edged sword of light! We are armed with the weapons of light.

In Colossians 3:3 Paul writes to the church, "...your life is hid with Christ in God." Let me illustrate both how we are hid in Christ and the mystery of the Trinity with the following example: Imagine three burning candles. Place the wicks together and you have one flame. Where does one fire end and the other begin? They are indistinguishable. They are one. Now separate them and they are again three flames.

Likewise, our lives are hid with Christ in God. Proverbs 20:27 says, "The spirit of man is the candle of the LORD...." God ignited us with the fire of the Holy Spirit. As we are in Him, our flame is indistinguishable from His flame. His flame engulfs our flame. Like the burning bush, we are not consumed. We are in Him, and He is in us.

"...When thou walkest through the fire, thou shalt not be burned; neither shall the flame kindle upon thee" (Isa. 43:2). Another mystery is solved: Fire cannot burn fire!

The luminous blood of Jesus resides within us, and we radiate as Christ did in this world. To evil spirits, we look just like Jesus. Their vision cannot penetrate the light of His blood. Unless we give ourselves away by behaving unlike Jesus, they cannot distinguish us, sons of God, from Him, the Son of God.

Surely one drop of His blood is enough to blind all the devils in hell! We are covered. Why should we run from the devil or his demons? Let the demons run from us!

The following story came from the mission field of Haiti. A Haitian voodoo priest was weaving a spell over a small band of superstitious people. The hour was midnight. The place was a deserted street in Port au Prince. This voodoo priest imagined himself to be an extremely powerful man of black magic. He was in league with the devil, and his spectators were mesmerized. As the dark priest performed his evil incantations, he noticed he was losing his grip on his captive audience. Something else was drawing their attention. He looked up to see what was challenging his authority.

To his surprise, he saw a luminescent form in a large sphere of light coming steadily toward his group. The fainthearted fled from the mysterious light; then even the brave ones lost courage and followed the others into the shadows. Only the witch doctor remained, and he felt he had to remain to uphold his reputation.

As the light came closer, it became brighter. The witch doctor strained to peer into the defiant light to identify the form he saw within it. The light repulsed him, and his head snapped away from the brightness. He summoned all of his nerve and tried again, but he had no power over the light. His magic was not working. He fell prostrate before the luminous form and began to whimper and beg for mercy. It was a public and shameful defeat.

From the pavement, he squinted up into the light to at last see the powerful being that had challenged him and won. He was surprised to see it was just a little old Christian lady walking home from an evening prayer meeting, praising God.

Hidden With Christ in God

The Lord is the light of our life. Demons are afraid of us because we are hid with Christ in God, in His light. The devil cannot penetrate that light, so he doesn't know who is inside: whether it is you, me, or Jesus! To the devil, we are the same person! That light is our armor, our helmet, and our breastplate! The devil is powerless.

Once I was in my study in our church in Tulsa. My son came in and said, "Daddy, there is a man I think you ought to come and check on."

I asked, "Has he been drinking?" Something told me he had.

"I don't know, Daddy." He had never really seen a drunk man.

"All right, I'll check on him after a while." I wasn't in a hurry to go. I knew in my spirit what was out there. I always know when the devil comes to visit. Sometimes the doorbell rings and I think, *There he is!*

Finally, one of the deacons came in and said, "Brother Huggins, there's a man out here. I think you'd better check on him now."

I said, "Yes, I guess I'd better." When I walked out of my office, I wasn't totally prepared for what I saw. There sat a swarthy, dirty man. He was hunched forward, rocking from side to side, with his hands between his knees. Foam was dripping out his mouth onto the floor. Around his neck was a scar about five inches long with huge stitch marks. It looked like something from a horror movie. Part of his ear had either been shot off or bitten off. He had scars all over his hands and tattoos on his knuckles. He looked evil and even smelled evil!

He glared at me with wide, predatory eyes. I didn't want him to think I was afraid, so I sat down beside him thinking that would be a bold thing to do. He tensed all over. The veins in his neck and forehead bulged and throbbed. He clenched his fists open and closed, until his knuckles turned white, while grinding his teeth so loudly it seemed they might break off.

He growled in a deep, raspy voice, "I'm the devil!"

I looked directly into his glassy eyes and calmly said, "Well, I'm Jesus." Now don't get excited and accuse me of sacrilege. Jesus said we could use His name, didn't He? I am hid with Christ in God. He is in me, the hope of glory.

I wasn't about to tell that demonized man that a nervous Larry Huggins is inside the armor of light, fighting the urge to run! That would give me away. So I boldly used Jesus' name.

Then I calmly reached over and laid my hand on the wretched man's shoulder. He instantly collapsed into my arms and wept like a baby. He totally surrendered because the irresistible blood of Jesus was upon me! I ministered deliverance to him and sent him peacefully on his way.

As believers, wherever we go, the Light of the world goes. As Jesus said, *"Ye are the light of the world..."* (Matt. 5:14). We are engulfed in light.

YOU ARE THE LIGHT OF THE WORLD

If you walk out of your home tonight and get into your car, all the devil will see is a ball of fire. In the spirit world, in the sight of the angels and demons, there is pure light beaming out of you, illuminating your automobile. As you drive down the road, that light shines forth into the spiritual darkness brighter than your headlights shine forth into the physical darkness.

From God's viewpoint in heaven, a dark sedan is going this way, and another dark sedan is going that way.

Suddenly down the road comes a ball of holy fire! "There goes one of my children!" says the Lord.

When you enter your house, say, "Thank God, the blood of Jesus is upon this house." Your house is lit up! Later that evening, the lights in the neighborhood begin to flicker out. One after the other, the houses go dark. You turn off your lights, but your house keeps shining brightly because you are a child of light! A believer lives in your house, and believers are never in the dark.

The adversary prowls around in the shadows, "seeking whom he may devour" (1 Peter 5:8). Evil spirits slip through the atmospheric heaven, looking for victims. Divorce is trying to enter one home. Strife is trying to enter another. Cancer is prowling here. Madness is lurking there. Adultery is searching for an open door.

Evil cannot visit your home if your home is full of light. The powers of darkness cannot penetrate the light. The bloodline drawn around your home is a line Satan cannot cross.

"In him was life; and the life was the light of men" (John 1:4). You are a child of light (Eph. 5:8). "Ye are the light of the world..." (Matt. 5:14).

This was the revelation Satan didn't want you to have. Now you know how utterly powerless he is when it comes to the blood of Jesus. What are you going to do with this knowledge? As it says in Revelation 12:11, you are going to overcome him by the blood of the Lamb and the word of your testimony.

WE PLEAD THE BLOOD

As we stand before the Supreme Judge, in the high court of heaven, we must each enter our plea. We have all sinned and come short of the glory of God.[4] Shall we plead guilty? That wouldn't be advised. Someone has already paid for the crime. How then shall we plead? "Your Honor, I PLEAD THE BLOOD OF JESUS!"

All these years, the church has been pleading the blood of Jesus without fully understanding what we were doing. When we plead the blood of Jesus, we are submitting to the courts of heaven the evidence of our new, pure bloodline as proof of our innocence.

By virtue of the new birth, we have been given a brand-new identity. We have received God's spiritual DNA. How can a new man, whose blood doesn't even match the old man's blood, be convicted of a crime? The case is airtight. We stand acquitted by irrefutable, blood evidence.

1 JOHN 1:7

7   But if we walk in the light, as he is in the light...the blood of Jesus Christ his Son cleanseth us from all sin.

CHAPTER 5

God's View of the Blood

So far we have dealt with what the blood of Jesus means to humanity and what it means to powers of darkness. Now let's consider God's view of redemption. What does the blood of Jesus mean to the heavenly Father?

Most of the sermons on the blood of Jesus have centered on what the blood means to the believer. There is a great deal of teaching available to us today about the blood covenant and the legal benefits of the blood. That is extremely important to know, but that is usually as far as it goes.

There definitely is a legal side to redemption. Our covenant with God is legal, binding, and ratified by the blood of Jesus Christ. It is a blood covenant. The Bible is a legal book, and therefore, it is binding, both upon us and upon God. Whatsoever things are bound on earth are also bound in heaven. (Matt. 16:19.)

The shedding of blood has always sanctioned God's covenants. Even the covenant of circumcision drew blood. Blood sealed the deal. For example, without shedding of blood is no remission of sin. (Heb. 9:22.) That side of redemption: the legal side.

There is more to redemption than just *legalities*. There are other realities. This book is really about the *vital* side of redemption. By vital, I mean that which is alive and pertains to life.

As Paul wrote to the Corinthians concerning the Law, "...the letter killeth, but the spirit giveth life" (2 Cor. 3:6). We must bear witness to the legal issues of the Word, but we also must recognize the life-issues. After all, the Word of God is alive.

It is one thing to have the right to live a good life. It's another to *enjoy* the good life. Just like it's one thing to be a hearer of the Word, but another to be a doer of the Word. Some know the Word and others *live* in the Word. There are laws and there are life principles. I am talking about life principles.

If we are to truly understand the blood of Jesus in its fullness, we must realize not only what it means to us as believers, but also what it means to the Father God. No one has paid a higher price than He has. No one places a greater value on the blood of Jesus than the Father does.

GOD FORGETS SIN

HEBREWS 10:16,18,19,22,23

16 This is the covenant that I will make with them after those days, saith the Lord, I will put my laws into their hearts, and in their minds will I write them; [17]and their sins and iniquities will I remember no more.

18 Now where remission of these is, there is no more offering for sin.

19 Having therefore, brethren, boldness to enter into the holiest by the blood of Jesus, [20]by a new and living way, which he [Jesus] hath consecrated for us, through the veil, that is to say, his flesh; [21]and having an high priest over the house of God;

22 Let us draw near with a true heart in full assurance of faith, having our hearts sprinkled from an evil conscience, and our bodies washed with pure water.

23 Let us hold fast the profession of our faith without wavering; (for he is faithful that promised...).

The number one thing that violates people's faith is remembrance of the past. Condemnation is the devil's favorite tool. In your case, like most, it is probably your memories of past failures and disappointments that keep you from enjoying God's highest and best.

Paul said, "...this one thing I do, forgetting those things which are behind, and reaching forth unto those things which are before" (Phil. 3:13).

We don't need to be reminded of our mistakes. Those who preach condemnation annoy me. Some preachers think they are helping people by dredging up their past. Those things don't need to be dug up. Leave them under the blood! God has forgiven you. You must forgive yourself.

The Bible tells us, "...If any man be in Christ, he is a new creature:" [altogether a new creation, a new type of being] "old things are passed away; behold, all things are become new" (2 Cor. 5:17). By the blood of Jesus we have become a new creation, and a new spirit has been recreated inside us. Unfortunately, we still have the same mind, and that old mind easily remembers all of our past failures.

Even our body has a certain amount of intelligence of its own; it remembers things. It remembers pleasure in sin. (Heb. 11:25.) It remembers pain. It has certain tastes and appetites. It craves some things and avoids other things.

The way we deal with our bodies is to yield our bodies unto God. Present your bodies "...a living sacrifice, holy, acceptable unto God, which is your reasonable service" (Rom. 12:1).

We *renew our minds* (v. 2) with the Word of God. Don't fall into Satan's trap of remembrance. Don't keep going back into the dark failures of your past. Once your sins are under the blood, God does not revisit them and neither should you.

Notice again what He said concerning the covenant He will make with His people "after those days": I will be their God and they will be My people. He will put His statutes in their hearts, and in their minds He will write them. He will remember their iniquities no more. (Heb. 10:16.) With this covenant, other scriptures tell us He said, "...I will be to them a God, and they shall be to me a people" (Heb. 8:10).

Let's not remind God of something He chose to forget. Think about it for a moment. God has chosen to forget our sins and iniquities. He says, "I will remember them no more." If words mean anything, this should tell us that God doesn't want us reminding Him of something He has consciously, deliberately determined to forget!

God has already forgiven us of all our sins, but most people have not forgiven themselves. Religion hasn't helped. It exacerbates the problem. How many times have you heard, "We are but worms and mere sinners, saved by grace."

No, we're not! Not since the blood of Jesus was applied to our lives. We *were* sinners, but *now* we are the children of God. Yes, my old man was a sinner. He had bad blood, spiritually speaking. But that old man is dead, and I am now a child of God.

You may ask, "What if we miss it?" Well, children do miss it, but they don't stop being children. My sons miss it every now and then. They may make mistakes and disappoint me, but they don't cease from being my children. They might lose out in fellowship, but they don't lose out in relationship.

My children have my blood in their veins. They are flesh of my flesh and bone of my bone. Even when they miss it, they are still mine.

We may miss it, but we are still God's children. We're born of His Spirit and washed in His blood. We were born not "of the will of the flesh, nor of the will of man, but of God" (John 1:13).

You are not a mere sinner, saved by grace. Some pious individual started that, no doubt—a religious "worm for Jesus" that thought it sounded humble. It is not humble. It is arrogant and proud to doubt the redemptive work of Christ.

True humility is saying the same thing that God says about you whether you feel like it or not. If He says that I am the righteousness of God, then I am the righteousness of God. (2 Cor. 5:21.) Period!

Here is the miracle of redemption. Not only does God forgive us of our sins, He does something we ourselves find almost impossible to do. He *forgets* our sins! He said of our sins and iniquities that He would *remember* them no more.

How can God—the creator of the universe, who knows each of the trillions of stars by name and has numbered the hairs of our head, who keeps inventory of every sparrow—forget anything? How can an omniscient, all-knowing, all-seeing God forget?

I've heard many lamentations from people who say things like, "I know you say that God forgets, but I can't forget. I know what an awful sinner I've been. Just the other day I did it again. I didn't mean to, and I've asked God to forgive me for it, but I just feel so bad. I feel like my prayers aren't being answered. I'm afraid to go to God because He is going to remember what I did. I just can't go to Him and say, 'Oh, God, it's me again, standing in the need of prayer.'"

People go through this all the time, and that is what hinders their prayers. Their hearts are condemned, and they have no confidence to approach God.

Hebrews 11:6 explains, "Without faith it is impossible to please him: for he that cometh to God must believe that he is, and that he is a rewarder of them that diligently seek him."

Sin-consciousness, or sin-remembrance, is a device Satan uses to hinder our fellowship with God. Memories of past failures rob us of future success.

1 JOHN 3:20,21; 1 JOHN 5:14,15

20 If our heart condemn us, God is greater than our heart, and knoweth all things.

21 Beloved, if our heart condemn us not, then have we confidence toward God....

14 And this is the confidence that we have in him, that, if we ask any thing according to his will, he heareth us:

15 And if we know that he hear us, whatsoever we ask, we know that we have the petitions that we desired of him.

We can come before God with confidence because "if we confess our sins, he is faithful and just to forgive us our sins, and to cleanse us from all unrighteousness" (1 John 1:9).

Once that sin is forgiven, it is forgotten!

But again I ask, "How can God forget anything, much less forget sin?" He has not just chosen to forget our sin, but He actually cannot remember our sin because of "...him that loved us, and washed us from our sins in his own blood" (Rev. 1:5).

THE BLOOD SPEAKS

Keep in mind that in the beginning God created man, Adam, and breathed life into him. He breathed it into his nostrils, but it went right into his blood because the life of all flesh is in the blood. When Adam committed sin, his blood was polluted with a curse, the curse of sin.

GENESIS 4:1,2,4,5

1 And Adam knew Eve, his wife, and she conceived, and bare Cain, and said, I have gotten a man from the LORD.

2 And she again bare his brother Abel. And Abel was a keeper of sheep, but Cain was a tiller of the ground. ³And in process of time it came to pass, that Cain brought of the fruit of the ground an offering unto the LORD.

4 And Abel, he also brought of the firstlings of his flock and of the fat thereof. And the LORD had respect unto Abel and to his offering:

> 5 But unto Cain and his offering he had not respect. And
> Cain was very wrath, and his countenance fell.

Abel's sacrifice was his dearest possession. It was a lamb, the firstling of his flock, without spot or blemish. He brought it to God as a sacrifice. Cain brought fruit and herbs or something of that nature as his sacrifice; but it was bloodless, even common.

When I was about eleven years old, I had a special pet. While the other kids had dogs or cats for pets, I had a baby goat. My little goat was sweet. I called her Nanny. She followed me everywhere I went, just like a puppy. Sometimes she would put her head against my leg and nudge me to pet her. She loved having her head scratched. We even went camping together. She slept outside my pup tent, and if anything came near she would sound the alarm, "Naahh, naahh!"

I loved my little goat. But my parents didn't. They thought she was a nuisance. Mom and Dad agreed, "Son, we need to get rid of that goat. She chews up everything. Whenever we open the door, she runs straight into the house." If we tried to tie her up, she would chew through the rope. She was into everything.

They said, "Son, we're going to give Nanny to some folks who have a ranch. She will be happier there. She will have room to roam around and play. She will be with other goats. She will not bother anyone. She'll really be happier." They finally convinced me it would be best for everyone, including Nanny, if she went to the ranch to live.

A few weeks later I discovered that those people had barbecued my goat and eaten her! I said to my parents, "They barbecued my goat! Dear God, you didn't tell me they were going to barbecue her!"

In the light of that, can you understand what Abel must have experienced when he brought the firstling of his flock, the one he loved best, to God? He probably loved that little lamb like I loved little Nanny.

Allow me to embellish this story. God said, "My sons, come into my presence and worship Me. Bring Me an offering."

For Able that meant the thing that was dearest to him.

Cain just pulled a few crops out of his field to take to God.

Abel asked himself, sincerely, *How much do I really love God?* And He went to his sheepfold to choose a lamb. At first, he chose a lame sheep, then thought, *Oh, God, I love You so much. You are so good to me. I can't offer You a lame sheep.* Then he culled a spotted sheep, but his heart said, *No, that's not your best.*

Abel stopped looking and somberly called out to his prized lamb, "Fluffy! Fluffy, where are you?" This was the most precious sheep he had, the one he loved the most.

"Yes, there you are, my friend." Nearby, on a green hill stood an exquisite, snow-white ram. His wool was softer, purer, and thicker than all the sheep. His horns curled

back around and pointed forward again. His hooves sparkled. He was beautiful and perfect.

The ewes and other lambs flocked around this one. He was the *progenitor* of his herd, the breeding stock.

Upon hearing his name, the noble ram walked through the flock and stood faithfully beside his shepherd. Abel stooped down, ran his fingers into the wool of Fluffy's neck and pulled his tender cheek up to his one last time.

Abel's tears streamed down his cheeks as he cut the ram's throat, bled it, and then offered his sacrifice unto God.

No wonder God had respect for Abel's offering. It was precious. That lamb's blood was proof of Abel's love.

But God did not respect Cain's common, bloodless offering.

GENESIS 4:6,8-10

6   And the LORD said unto Cain, Why art thou wroth? and why is thy countenance fallen? ⁷If thou doest well, shalt thou not be accepted? and if thou doest not well, sin lieth at the door. [It certainly did, and it still does!] And unto thee shall be his desire, and thou shalt rule over him.

8   And Cain talked with Abel his brother: and it came to pass, when they were in the field, that Cain rose up against Abel his brother, and slew him.

9   And the LORD said unto Cain, Where is Abel thy brother? And he said, I know not: Am I my brother's keeper?

10   And he said, What hast thou done? the voice of thy brother's blood crieth unto me from the ground. ¹¹And now

> art thou cursed from the earth, which hath opened her
> mouth to receive thy brother's blood from thy hand.

Cain heard the voice of an angry God. The Judge of the universe demanded, "Where is your brother? The voice of his blood cries out to Me from the ground."

Notice there was a quality of life in Abel's blood that even from the ground it spoke so unmistakably that God in heaven heard it. Blood speaks.

The voice of Abel's blood came up before God, the Lawgiver who gave us the Old Testament, the same God who commanded, "Eye for eye, tooth for tooth, hand for hand, foot for foot," "life for life."[1]

The blood of Abel accused Cain. In court we need the testimony of a witness. In the courts of heaven the testimony of Abel's blood was a witness against Cain. His blood cried out for justice.

THE OLD COVENANT

Later in history, God gave us a covenant through Moses. Before there was a new covenant based upon better promises there was an old covenant.

Jesus ushered in the new covenant. "...The days come, saith the LORD, that I will make a new covenant with the house of Israel, and with the house of Judah" (Jer. 31:31). The days we are living in are "the days" that "come." As we have seen, in the new covenant, God writes His laws on our hearts and in our minds and remembers our sins and iniquities no more. In the new covenant there is no remembrance of sins, whatsoever.

However, in the old covenant there was the continual remembrance of sin. In fact, the rituals, which the high priest performed annually, served only to postpone God's judgment. You see, Israel served an angry God, a God of justice, a God who punished sin. The blood of their sacrifices bought them reprieve twelve months at a time. There was a continual awareness of sin.

In the ninth chapter of Hebrews there is a description of the earthly tabernacle, which was a replica of the heavenly tabernacle:

HEBREWS 9:1,3,6,7

1   Then verily the first covenant had also ordinances of divine service, and a worldly sanctuary. ²For there was a tabernacle made; the first, wherein was the candlestick, and the table, and the shewbread; which is called the sanctuary.

3   And after the second veil, the tabernacle which is called the Holiest of all; ⁴which had the golden censer, and the ark of the covenant overlaid round about with gold, wherein was the golden pot that had manna, and Aaron's rod that budded, and the tables of the covenant; ⁵and over it the cherubims of glory shadowing the mercyseat; of which we cannot now speak particularly.

6   Now when these things were thus ordained, the priests went always into the first tabernacle, accomplishing the service of God.

7   But into the second went the high priest alone once every
     year, not without blood, which he offered for himself, and
     for the errors of the people.

In the earthly tabernacle, if the high priest were to go
into the Holy of Holies without blood, he would immediately die. He couldn't come into the presence of God
uncovered. No one can stand before God without blood.

We can see this in the very important example of the
Passover when God used lambs' blood to save the
Israelites from destruction. God instructed the families of
Israel living in the bondage of Egypt to sacrifice a
passover lamb without blemish, a male of the first year;
dip a bunch of hyssop in a basin of its blood; and strike
the lintel and side posts of their houses.

When the Lord saw the blood, He passed over their
doors and did not suffer the destroyer to go into their
houses to smite them. Because of that blood, the Israelites
were spared when the firstborn of both man and beast in
Egypt were slain. (Exod. 12:5,12,13,21-23.)

Some think they will get to heaven by burning
incense. I am sorry to say, smoke won't get them into the
presence of God. Some think they will get to heaven by
chanting. Noise won't work either. Others think they will
get to heaven through their good works. Wrong again! No
soul can enter heaven without the application of the
blood of atonement.

Once a year the high priest cautiously went into the
presence of God with fear and trembling to offer the

atoning blood sacrifices for his sin and the sin of his house and for the sin of the people. He put on his priestly garment decorated around the hem with pomegranates and bells between them that made a jingling noise as he walked. (Exod. 28:33-35.)

Before going into the Holy of Holies, he purified himself very, *very* carefully.[2] Inside the Holy of Holies (the Most Holy Place within the veil—Exod. 26:33,34), he sprinkled the blood of a young bullock, the sacrifice for his sin and that of his house, and the blood of a goat, the sacrifice for the sin of the children of Israel, on the mercy seat. (Lev. 16:2-19,34.) This application of blood, with the other actions of the day, made atonement for his sins and for the sins of the people for one more year.

If the priest was unworthy, he suffered fatal consequences. The instructions God gave to consecrate and purify the priests and the actions the priests should take when ministering to Him were to be followed exactly so that the priests would "die not." For example, Exodus 28:35 says of the bells around the hem of Aaron's robe (vv. 33-35) that were heard when Aaron went into the Holy of Holies: "And it shall be upon Aaron to minister: and his sound shall be heard when he goeth in unto the holy place before the LORD, and when he cometh out, that he die not."

In Leviticus 10:1-2 we see an example of the consequences when two of Aaron's sons did not follow the Lord's directions in detail. They offered strange fire before the Lord, which the Lord had commanded them not to do, and as a result, they died!

HEBREWS 9:8,9

8   The Holy Ghost this signifying, that the way into the holiest of all was not yet made manifest, while as the first tabernacle was yet standing:

9   Which was a figure for the time then present, in which were offered both gifts and sacrifices, that could not make him that did the service perfect, as pertaining to the conscience.

Under that covenant, people never forgot that they were sinners. Although they offered the blood of bulls and goats, year after year, they never forgot their sins. The blood of bulls and goats, while covering up their sins, did not make them perfect, as pertaining to the conscience.

HEBREWS 9:10,11

10   Which stood only in meats and drinks, and divers washings, and carnal ordinances, imposed on them until the time of reformation.

11   But Christ being come an high priest of good things to come, by a greater and more perfect tabernacle, not made with hands, that is to say, not of this building.

The "greater and more perfect tabernacle"? It is stretched in heaven, where God is. There is a heavenly Holy of Holies where Jesus, our High Priest of the New Testament, entered with His own blood to make eternal atonement for us.

HEBREWS 9:12

12 Neither by the blood of goats and calves, but by his own blood he entered in once into the holy place, having obtained eternal redemption for us.

Heaven is an awesome and important place. Yet, no matter what is going on in our lives, heaven is aware of it. Why is it then we are not more aware of heaven? We ought to see things from heaven's point of view. As Paul said, "Set your affection on things above, not on things on the earth" (Col. 3:2).

A NEW COVENANT

Jesus didn't enter that Holy of Holies with the blood of bulls or calves. He entered, as our High Priest, into heaven's holiest place with *His* own *blood.*

HEBREWS 9:13,14

13 For if the blood of bulls and of goats, and the ashes of an heifer sprinkling the unclean, sanctifieth to the purifying of the flesh:

14 how much more shall the blood of Christ, who through the eternal Spirit offered himself without spot to God, purge your conscience from dead works to serve the living God?

In order to walk in victory, we must purge our conscience from dead works. We must be reminded that God not only forgives, but He also forgets. We too should forget. Some would rather do penance for their sins. But penance doesn't help you forget sin. It helps you remember sin. Some think good deeds offset bad deeds. Wrong! What can wash away sin? Nothing but the blood of Jesus!

Salvation is not just forgiveness of sins. It is restoration to sonship with all the rights and privileges of royalty.

HEBREWS 9:15-17

15 And for this cause he is the mediator of the new testament, that by means of death, for the redemption of the transgressions that were under the first testament, they which are called might receive the promise of eternal inheritance.

16 For where a testament is, there must also of necessity be the death of the testator.

17 For a testament is of force after men are dead: otherwise it is of no strength at all while the testator liveth.

God left you an inheritance. The Bible is actually the last will and testament of Jesus Christ. Jesus is the *Testator.* You are an heir. You were written in the will that Jesus died to ratify.

HEBREWS 9:19,21,23

19 For when Moses had spoken every precept to all the people according to the law, he took the blood of calves and of goats, with water, and scarlet wool, and hyssop, and sprinkled both the book, and all the people,

20 saying, This is the blood of the testament which God hath enjoined unto you.

21 Moreover he sprinkled with blood both the tabernacle, and all the vessels of the ministry.

22 And almost all things are by the law purged with blood; and without shedding of blood is no remission.

23 It was therefore necessary that the patterns of things in the heavens should be purified with these; but the heavenly things themselves with better sacrifices than these.

What a remarkable statement! The heavenly utensils of worship had to be cleansed *"with better sacrifices than these"* (v. 23). Evidently, Adam's sin reached all the way to heaven because we read here that the vessels in heaven had to be *purified* with a better sacrifice than that of bulls and goats: the blood of Jesus.

THE BLOOD OF THE LAMB

HEBREWS 9:24-27

24 For Christ is not entered into the holy places made with hands, which are the figures of the true; but into heaven itself, now to appear in the presence of God for us:

25 Nor yet that he should offer himself often, as the high priest entereth into the holy place every year with blood of others;

26 For then must he often have suffered since the foundation of the world: but now once in the end of the world hath he appeared to put away sin by the sacrifice of himself.

27 And as it is appointed unto men once to die, but after this the judgment.

Let's review again. "It is appointed unto men once to die, but after this the judgment" (v. 27). Jesus made one sacrifice, and it was enough. In Moses' day the high priest made sacrifices every year, but that wasn't enough. The people kept remembering their transgressions and sins. Jesus went in only once and God forgot every sin.

First Peter 1:18-19 says that we were not redeemed with corruptible things, such as silver and gold, but by the precious blood of Jesus, as of a lamb without blemish or spot.

The more rare a thing is, the more precious it is. Someone once gave me a gold coin that was no bigger than the tip of my finger, but it was precious because it was rare. It is true that the fewer there are of certain things, the more valuable they become.

Jesus' blood was the only blood on this earth that came from heaven. The most expensive perfumes from France cost more than those from a discount department store because they are imported. Jesus' blood was imported from heaven! It is extraordinary, rare, and costly. It is the precious blood of the Lamb.

When God sacrificed Jesus, the most precious of all blood was shed. It hurt the Father to see His Son lose even one drop of blood. God didn't relish seeing Jesus suffer, but it had to be done. His blood was an offering for our sin. His love for us compelled Him to sacrifice Jesus.

We fathers would rather suffer for our children than see them suffer. Perhaps you can understand how precious a son's blood is to his father if you consider Abraham's willingness to sacrifice his son, Isaac. It was precious blood he was asked to spill.

One day I came home from work and noticed that the garage door was open. I became angry because I knew that my six-year-old son, Forest, had been in the garage, although I had told him not to go in there.

I am a sculptor and have expensive tools. I keep my cutting tools razor sharp because a dull tool is unsafe. I had constantly warned my son never to play with Daddy's tools. They are dangerous.

Forest disobeyed me. He had been playing with my tools and left the garage door open. I thought, *Anyone could just walk in and help himself to my tools.* Then I saw something shiny on the garage floor and said to myself, "There's one of my tools. That little rascal has dropped one of my chisels on the floor. If it's damaged, I'm going to tan his hide! In fact, I'll tan it anyway because he didn't mind me."

I walked in and picked up my chisel, expecting it to be chipped. It's not easy to put a sharp edge on a chipped tool. I examined it and saw that it was indeed chipped, but then I saw something else. I dropped the chisel, not caring if it broke. There was blood on the blade!

I saw a drop of blood on the floor, then another—I ran into the house, following the trail of blood, calling out, "Forest! Forest! Son, where are you?"

Blood was spattered on the floor, the walls and even the ceiling, from him slinging his wounded hand in pain. I found him in the bathroom, holding his thumb. It was split down the end, through the thumbnail, all the way to the bone. Blood was streaming out of it, and he was sobbing in pain. Don't you hurt when your children hurt?

I felt so bad when I saw him. I said, "Oh, son, I'm so sorry!" He was more frightened of me than he was the wound. He cried, "I'm sorry, Daddy. Please don't spank me. I didn't mean to drop it, Daddy. I'm sorry."

"Son, don't worry. Daddy's not angry with you. This is why I told you not to play with those tools, because something like this could happen. I'm not going to punish you." Oh, yes, I had been angry all right. But when I saw my son's blood, all anger left me.

I found gauze and disinfectant. I took Forest over to the sink and told him, "Now don't look at the blood," but I looked at it.

I can't tell you how it made me feel as I watched my son's blood running down the drain. It seemed to be pulling my heart out. This was my blood, his father's blood, dripping down the drain.

I talked to Forest soothingly while I gently washed his thumb, cleaned the cut with hydrogen peroxide, and dried it off with a piece of sterile cotton. Then I applied disinfectant to it, bandaged it with gauze, made a little splint for it, and fastened it with adhesive tape.

When I was done, I said a prayer for healing, gave him a little kiss, and wiped the last tear from his eye.

He let out a sigh and looked up at me, "Oh, Daddy," he said. "I think you need to stop being a preacher and become a doctor for little kids!"

If my son's blood is precious to me, how much more precious is the blood of Jesus to the heavenly Father? Jesus went into the Holy of Holies with His own blood and presented it before His Father. How did God look upon that blood? What did it mean to the One who spoke from heaven saying, "...This is my beloved Son, in whom I am well pleased" (Matt. 3:17)?

THE HEAVENLY TABERNACLE

I have tried to paint you a picture of the earthly tabernacle. Now let's paint a picture of heaven. Let's go right up to the throne room where God sits.

HEBREWS 12:18-21

18 For ye are not come unto the mount that might be touched, and that burned with fire, nor unto blackness, and darkness, and tempest,

19 And the sound of a trumpet, and the voice of words; which voice they that heard intreated that the word should not be spoken to them any more:

20 (For they could not endure that which was commanded, And if so much as a beast touch the mountain, it shall be stoned, or thrust through with a dart:

21 And so terrible was the sight, that Moses said, I exceedingly fear and quake...).

This is a picture of the mountain to which Moses went to receive the law and the pattern for the tabernacle. There was fire on the mountain as the Lord descended, and the whole mountain shook. (Ex. 19:18.) There were awesome thunders, lightning, and darkness. Then God's voice spoke, and it was so terrible that the people cried out, "Moses, you go talk to God. We're afraid!" (Ex. 20:18,19).

That place was so holy that God pronounced a death penalty upon anyone, or any beast, who so much as touched the foot of the mountain. Surely the people thought, *God is a God of judgment and wrath. We are unworthy. We have murmured and complained. We cannot go onto the mountain, face-to-face with God.*

HEBREWS 12:21

21 And so terrible was the sight, that Moses said, I exceedingly fear and quake...).

Moses was dreadfully afraid when he had to go up into the mountain and stand in the presence of the Almighty, but that sight wasn't as awesome as the heavenly mount Zion.

HEBREWS 12:22,23

22 But ye are come unto mount Sion, and unto the city of the living God, the heavenly Jerusalem, and to an innumerable company of angels,

23 To the general assembly and church of the firstborn, which are written in heaven, and to God the Judge of all, and to the spirits of just men made perfect.

We have come before God.

We have come, not to an earthly mountain or to a man-made tabernacle (that was fearful enough). But, as the writer said, we have come into to the *actual* Mount

Zion, to the *real* heavenly Jerusalem, not to the replica, but into the actual city!

Positionally, we are in the presence of the Living God, "And [He] hath raised us up together, and made us sit together in heavenly places in Christ Jesus" (Eph. 2:6). We are among the cloud of witnesses (Heb. 12:1) and in the presence of an innumerable host of angels.

Cherubim surround the mercy seat as they do the earthly replica.[3] There on the throne sits God Himself.[4] Before Him are the elders with their crowns.[5] Among the smoke there are four beasts with eyes around their heads, winged creatures, giving glory and honor and thanksgiving unto God.[6] Lightnings and thunderings are proceeding from the throne[7] as voices cry, "...Holy, holy, holy, Lord God Almighty, which was, and is, and is to come."[8]

This is the most awesome of sights. It is truly a fearful thing to fall into the hands of the Living God! There sits the Most High God, the Self-Existent One, the Omnipotent Ruler of the Universe. With one breath, He can destroy the world. By raising a finger, He can split the earth. With one word, He can extinguish the stars.

There He is sitting on His judgment seat, in the real tabernacle, and that's where we have come, into the presence of "...God, the judge of all, and to the spirits of just men made perfect, And to Jesus the mediator of the new covenant, and to the blood of sprinkling, that speaketh better things than that of Abel" (Heb. 12:23,24).

LIFE IN JESUS

Abel's blood must have cried out to Jehovah, "Avenge me, O God! I sacrificed to you. I lived righteously, and I was unfairly slain by my wicked brother. Avenge me, O Holy Father!" Abel's blood demanded justice, and God heard it.

Would not the God who was moved by Abel's blood be moved by His Son's blood? How could God restrain Himself while Jesus was mercilessly beaten and shamefully crucified? How could He hold back His fury? Why didn't He release His armies of angels? He was capable of intervening.

But God held Himself and His angels back. Perhaps as He restrained Himself, He again weighed humanity in the scales. *Are these unrighteous, unthankful, and unholy people worthy of My Son?* He let the events run their course.

You already know what happened in hell. Now you will learn what happened in heaven. Three days after Jesus was taken from the cross and entombed, He was resurrected.

Jesus briefly met Mary in route from the tomb to the throne. He said, "...Touch me not; for I am not yet ascended to my Father..." (John 20:17). He could not be defiled. He was on His way to present Himself unto God and enter the true Holy of Holies as our High Priest.

HEBREWS 9:24

24 For Christ is not entered into the holy places made with hands, which are the figures of the true; but into heaven itself, now to appear in the presence of God for us.

Imagine that suddenly into heaven's courts before God in the midst of His royal train, Jesus comes dressed in the robes of the High Priest! The thunder and lightning cease. The smoke stops boiling. The elders stop singing, the angels stand at attention, and the seraphim fold their wings. All is quiet.

Jesus, the Victor, the Passover Lamb of God sacrificed to take away the sin of the world,[9] strides confidently into the Holy Place. All eyes are upon Him. In His hands He holds a basin filled with His own precious blood. He takes hyssop, dips it into the blood, and sprinkles it on the candlestick, and the blood speaks! The blood speaks better things than that of Abel. It says, "Mercy!"

Then Jesus walks over to the table with the shewbread and covers it in blood, and the blood says, "Mercy!" He confidently strides into the Holy of Holies and sprinkles His blood upon the mercy seat, and the blood says, "Mercy!" He covers all the furnishings of the tabernacle with His own livid, luminous love—His blood. And His blood cries, "Mercy, mercy, MERCY!"

God the Father hears the blood, and it has an irresistible effect upon Him. His anger is assuaged as the voice of liquid love says, "Forgive them, Father. Have mercy!"

I can imagine the Father's eyes beholding His beloved Son who has just returned from conquering death and hell. Jesus gazes at Him and says, "The price has been paid Father. They are free. We've won!"

Oh, the blood of Jesus speaks better things than that of Abel. Abel's blood cried out for justice. Jesus' blood cries out for mercy and life. Jesus' blood sings a song of tender mercy and unconditional love:

PSALM 51:1,2

1   Have mercy upon me, O God, according to thy lovingkindness: according unto the multitude of thy tender mercies blot out my transgressions.

2   Wash me throughly from mine iniquity, and cleanse me from my sin.

The heavenly host takes up the new song. The heavens begin to ring with mercy: *"Mercy, Father. Mercy, mercy! Have mercy, Father. Mercy...."*

God's countenance softens. As He looks about, the blood eclipses all He sees. His eyes are irresistibly drawn to the brilliant light and crimson red of liquid love. He sees no sin. He sees no stain. How can He see beyond the blood? It arrests His gaze. It captures His attention. It has first place in His heart. The blood rings in His ears, "Mercy! Mercy! MERCY!"

From that day to this, even though Satan has been prosecuting our case, the Father doesn't listen to what he's saying, "But they've sinned! They have failed! They have broken the commandments! They've..." Try as he will, he cannot drown the sound of Jesus' blood, crying, "Mercy, mercy!"

Can't you imagine God saying, "I see his lips moving, but I can't hear a word he's saying!

What God does hear is, *"Mercy, mercy! MERCY! Mercy, mercy, mercy, MERCY!"*

The blood of Jesus speaks better things than that of Abel. And it's speaking yet for you: *"Forgive them Father; they don't know what they do."*

GOD'S VIEW OF THE BLOOD

The heavenly Holy of Holies is painted with the blood of Jesus. It's wallpapered, carpeted, and covered with the livid, luminous blood of Jesus. God thinks it is the most exquisite divine-materiality in the universe. God thinks we are precious and worthy, just as He intended from the beginning.

The Lamb of God, His own dear Son, was sacrificed for mankind, once and for all. When God looks at you and me, we are covered in the blood of Jesus. All He sees is the blood. All He hears is the blood. There is now no more remembrance of sin.

As we boldly enter His throne room, into the very presence of God our Father, we are clothed with the luminous blood of the Lamb. That blood intercedes on our behalf. We don't have to plead our case. We just plead the blood of Jesus, and the blood speaks for us.

You can never plead a better case than that which the blood of Jesus is pleading for you. Jesus Christ is the mediator of a new covenant. He is the High Priest of a better covenant based upon far better promises.

You don't have to go before God begging, "It's not my fault; I didn't know what I was doing; I'll never do it again...."

All you have to do is approach God in confidence and say, "Father, I plead the tender mercies of the Lord Jesus Christ. I'm washed in His blood. I repent of my wrongdoing and, according to Your Word, I am the righteousness of God in Christ."

God will say to you, "Come in, son. I do not remember anything bad. All I hear about you is good. Come in."

God's wrath was poured out at Calvary. Mercy now rejoices over judgment. His countenance is changed. He is saying to you, "Yes, you are My child. You have My blood. That is the blood that went from Me into Jesus and from Jesus into you. Yes, My child, come in. You are welcome here."

God can never again remember your sins and iniquities because the blood of Jesus speaks so compellingly that it demands the Father's attention. It's always in His ears. It's always before His eyes. It's always on His mind.

The blood puts everything into perspective. There are no big Christians or little Christians, no important Christians or unimportant Christians. There are only blood-bought sons of God. Some may occupy positions of higher responsibility in terms of public worship and ministry, but our only claim is that we are washed in blood of the Lamb. The blood covering makes us truly *special*.

If only we could fully comprehend the importance of Jesus' deed when He walked into the Holy of Holies as our High Priest and offered up, not the blood of bulls and goats, but His own priceless blood! Through His obedience, you and I have been returned to God's family and restored to sonship, "...Thou art my Son, this day have I begotten thee" (Acts 13:33). When He was raised up, we were raised up.

If I could, tonight while everyone sleeps, I would take a paintbrush and paint the whole world red. People would all wake up and find themselves painted blood red.

Then people would be reminded that, "God so loved the world, that He gave His only begotten Son, that whosoever believeth in him should not perish, but have everlasting life" (John 3:16).

Then they might begin to see the world as God does, covered in the blood. God gave His Son to die for this world, and He wants each of us to live every day of our lives remembering that the blood still speaks.

CHAPTER 6

What the Blood Says About You

As we have seen in Genesis 4:10, the blood of Abel cried to God from the ground. Hebrews 11:4 tells us that by his blood, Able *"yet speaketh"* (Heb. 11:4). The blood of Abel *yet speaketh.* If the blood of Abel is yet speaking today, then certainly the blood of Jesus is yet speaking today!

1 PETER 1:18,19

18 Forasmuch as ye know that ye were not redeemed with corruptible things, as silver and gold, from your vain conversation received by tradition from your fathers;

19 But with the precious blood of Christ, as of a lamb without blemish and without spot.

Hear what the blood is saying about you:

I am the Blood of Jesus. I am incorruptible. This means I can never be destroyed, depleted, or diminished in power. I am just as strong today as

I was two thousand years ago or ever before. I am working effectually for you right now.

I am the Blood of Redemption. I am more precious than silver and gold. I paid for your release from the prison of sin. I bought your freedom. I declare that you are hereby free. I proclaim loudly, before God, the saints of God, the angels of God, and even before the devils, you are God's peculiar treasure.

I am the Blood of Freedom. I say you are free. You are free from dead religion. You are free to worship the Living God in Spirit and in truth. I say bondage is never God's will for you. You shall live in liberty.

I am the Blood of Cleansing. I certify that you have been made spotless and whole. I proclaim that you have been completely cleansed. I say, "What God hath cleansed, no one can call unclean or common."

I am Precious Blood. I am dearer than money, cars, clothes, or houses. I am true treasure. I contain all the virtues and qualities of Jesus. Hear Me. Because I, the Blood of Christ, have been applied to your life, you are precious. Do not believe any words that say otherwise.

ROMANS 8:32-34

32 He that spared not his own Son, but delivered him up for us all, how shall he not with him also freely give us all things?

33 Who shall lay any thing to the charge of God's elect? It is God that justifieth.

34 Who is he that condemneth? It is Christ that died, yea rather, that is risen again, who is even at the right hand of God, who also maketh intercession for us.

I am the Blood of Intercession. God listens to Me as I speak on your behalf. I say you are special; He agrees. I say that you are bound to succeed. He agrees. I say you always win. He agrees. By Me, you cannot fail.

I am the Blood of Prosperity. Hear Me. I am true prosperity. I guarantee that God will never withhold any good thing from you. He gave Me, the Blood of His Son, His best. Now, with Me, He gladly lavishes good things upon you. I say you are rich.

I am the Blood of Sanctification. Jesus' body was raised from spiritual death through Me by God's power. I restored the Son of God unto newness of life. I sanctified Him even after He had become sin and a curse. I restored Him unto righteousness. I washed away the defilement of hell and consecrated His risen body to return to heaven. I have likewise consecrated you.

I am the Blood of Light. I say walk in the light as He is in the light and I, the Blood of Jesus, will cleanse you of every stain of sin. Abide in Me, child of light, and you will never walk in darkness again.

I am the Blood of Access. I certify that you have been approved to enjoy all the benefits of heaven, without restriction. I am your passport to the kingdom of God. I announce you as you enter His presence, "Hear ye! Hear ye! A royal son of God has arrived!"

REVELATION 5:9,10

9 …Thou art worthy…for thou wast slain, and hast redeemed us to God by thy blood out of every kindred, and tongue, and people, and nation;

10 and hast made us unto our God kings and priests: and we shall reign on the earth.

I am Royal Blood. I attest to your royal birthright. You are born into the tribe of Judah. I declare that you are a citizen of Zion, the heavenly city of God. I testify that you are a son of God in good standing. I have made you a prince.

I am the Blood of Dominion. I have been applied to your life and I have made you a king. Indeed, where the word of a king is there is power. By Me you rule and reign.

I am the Blood of Authority. I certify your dominion. I command that your word be respected. By Me you have commanding power. Whenever you desire anything that the Word promises, you can appropriate it by Me. I say you have kingdom authority. Thou shalt also decree a thing, and it shall be established unto thee: and the light shall shine upon thy ways.

EZEKIEL 16:6

6   And when I passed by thee, and saw thee polluted in thine own blood, I said unto thee when thou wast in thy blood, Live.

I am the Blood of Virtue. I pronounce you curse-free! When I was applied to your life, I imparted the very life and nature of God unto you. I am renewing your strength and your youth. I say you are empowered to live life to the fullest.

I am the Blood of Blessing. I say the virtue of heaven is in you. You have in your being the life that is stronger than death, stronger than disease, stronger than poverty, and stronger than sin. I profess you are too blessed to be cursed!

LEVITICUS 17:11

11   For the life of the flesh is in the blood.

I am the Blood of Healing. I am in you right now, imparting life and health to all your flesh. I say disease cannot stand in My presence. Evil spirits and darkness flee from Me. I say you are a vessel of God containing the treasure of divine life. For I will restore health unto thee, and I will heal thee of thy wounds.

JOHN 6:53

53   ...Verily, verily, I say unto you, Except ye eat the flesh of the
     Son of man, and drink his blood, ye have no life in you.

I am Sacred Blood. When you partake of the
Lord's Table, you partake of Me. I say you are
forgiven. I say you also have the power to forgive.
I say sin's curse has been broken. I say you also
have the power to break any curse.

I am the Blood of Communion. By Me you are
united with God in Holy Communion. I say you
are in the family of God. I say nothing whatsoever
can separate you from the love of God.

1 JOHN 1:7

7   But if we walk in the light, as he is in the light, we have
    fellowship one with another, and the blood of Jesus Christ
    his Son cleanseth us from all sin.

I am the Blood of Purification. I am life, and I am
light. I say you are filled with divine light right
now. I say you are in God's light, and His shines
through you. You have the right to live among the
children of light. Let no one say otherwise.

I am the Blood of Illumination. I say the light of
My blood is in you right now driving away spiritual darkness. You have no reason to fear evil. Evil
fears you. I say you will never dwell in darkness.
You are now in the Kingdom of Light. You are a
child of light and you will shine forever, as a star
in the heavens.

COLOSSIANS 1:13,14

13 Who hath delivered us from the power of darkness, and hath translated us into the kingdom of his dear Son:

14 In whom we have redemption through his blood, even the forgiveness of sins.

I am the Blood of Deliverance. I say the devil has no claim on you. I say you have been acquitted and released from the place where you were once held prisoner.

I am the Blood of Salvation. By Me you can live safe from all harm and free of all alarm. I say you are now a permanent resident of the Kingdom of Light. You are as far away from the devil's domain as light is from dark.

COLOSSIANS 1:20

20 And, having made peace through the blood of his cross, by him to reconcile all things unto himself; by him, I say, whether they be things in earth, or things in heaven.

I am the Blood of the Cross. I tipped the scales of justice in your favor. I have satisfied the courts of heaven. I say your account is balanced. I say your debt is paid in full. I say there are no outstanding claims against you. I say you are free from all warrants, liens, or summons.

HEBREWS 9:22

22 And almost all things are by the law purged with blood; and without shedding of blood is no remission.

I am the Blood of Cancellation. I proclaim your sins are cancelled. In an instant I cancelled all the disappointments and failures that you accumulated in your lifetime.

I am the Blood of Assurance. I say your past has passed. I say here before God stands a new creature. I say, "Hear Me! No one shall prevent this one from living the good life."

REVELATION 1:5

5   And from Jesus Christ, who is the faithful witness, and the first begotten of the dead, and the prince of the kings of the earth. Unto him that loved us, and washed us from our sins in his own blood.

I am the Blood of the Great King. Does anyone know His heart better than I? I say enjoy the protection of the King. I say enjoy the provision of the King. The King of Kings has made you a king. Wear your robes of red. Hold forth your scepter. Wear your golden crown.

I am the Blood of Inheritance. I testify that you are an heir of the royal inheritance. The King's estate is yours. You share all the rights of inheritance with Him. I say His will is now in effect because the Testator died (and He rose again). By Me you can claim your share of the eternal reward and enjoy it with your Lord because the Testator who died lives again.

HEBREWS 9:11,12

11 But Christ being come an high priest of good things to come, by a greater and more perfect tabernacle, not made with hands, that is to say, not of this building;

12 Neither by the blood of goats and calves, but by his own blood he entered in once into the holy place, having retained eternal redemption for us.

I am the Blood of Promise. It was I, the Blood of Jesus, who went into the holy presence of God for you. Heaven stood at attention as I ratified the new covenant, which is a far better covenant with far better promises than the old. I say your covenant benefits are available now and forever more.

I am the Blood of the Testament. I guarantee that you are a beneficiary of the new covenant. I promise all God has is yours, as all you have is His. I promise, you are welcome in His house, as He is welcome in your house. Do not allow anyone to deny you what I purchased for you.

I am the Blood of Abundance. I promise you a good life. I promise you long life. I promise you unconditional love. Superabundant life is yours right now, today. Do not settle for less.

HEBREWS 9:24-27

24 For Christ is not entered into the holy places made with hands, which are the figures of the true; but into heaven itself, now to appear in the presence of God for us:

25 Nor yet that he should offer himself often, as the high priest entereth into the holy place every year with blood of others;

26 For then must he often have suffered since the foundation of the world: but now once in the end of the world hath he appeared to put away sin by the sacrifice of himself.

27 And as it is appointed men once to die, but after this the judgment.

I am the Blood of Atonement. I have made you at one with God. I am the eternal sacrifice for sin. I am ever before God. There is no other sacrifice needed for sin. I settled the sin problem once and for all.

I am the Blood of Eternal Life. I say you have nothing to fear in death. You passed into life when you trusted in Me. You will someday simply step out of this place and into another. I assure that you have nothing to dread on that day.

I am the Blood of Warning. Tell others to heed. It will be a day of woe for those who have not placed their trust in Me. Without the blood of the Lamb, none can be saved. I say warn the wicked while it is still called today.

I am the Blood of Accessibility. I bid thee come! Behold, now is the accepted time. Behold, today is the day of salvation. Hear Me! No matter what you've done, come! While there is still time, come.

HEBREWS 12:23,24

23 To the general assembly and church of the firstborn, which are written in heaven, and to God the Judge of all, and to the spirits of just men made perfect,

24 And to Jesus the mediator of the new covenant, and to the blood of sprinkling, that speaketh better things than that of Abel.

I am the Blood of Grace. The old has passed away. No more eye for eye or life for life. By Me you have been judged righteous, not by works, but by faith. You cannot earn salvation. It's God's free gift.

I am the Blood of Expectation. I speak of tender mercies. I speak of everlasting favor. I speak amazing grace. I speak of no more sorrows. I speak of cloudless days. The Son will shine forever. Seedtime and harvest will not cease as long as the earth remains.

I am the Blood of Perfection. I have done a thorough work of remaking you in His image. Do not look upon the outer man. Look upon the inner man. Trust the New Birth. I say you are complete, perfect and entire, and you come behind in no good thing.

I am the Blood of Truth. Truth is all I speak. I have made you a lover of truth. With Me, the Blood of Christ, upon your heart, you will not be deceived. Speak the truth in love, and you'll be speaking the same with Me.

REVELATION 5:9,10

9 And they sung a new song, saying, Thou art worthy to take the book, and to open the seals thereof: for thou wast slain, and hast redeemed us to God by thy blood out of every kindred, and tongue, and people, and nation;

10 And hast made us unto our God kings and priests: and we shall reign on the earth.

I am the Blood of New Creation. You are no longer a mere unchained man. You are a brand-new species of being. You now walk upon this earth as the Second Adam, a true son of God.

I am the Blood of Heaven. I declare that by Me you have become a royal priest in this holy nation. You are a citizen of Zion and can now live as an ambassador of Christ. I decree you shall enjoy your diplomatic immunity and royal privilege, on earth as it is in heaven.

I am the Blood of Fidelity. I say what God says. You shall speak the language I speak. Hear ye! Hear ye! Hearken, sun, moon, stars, wind, waves, and sea. Listen, grass and trees. Listen, all you creatures. This child of God before you God has set here to rule by decree.

I am the Blood of the Seal. I have sealed the book. I have sealed the promises. I have sealed your salvation. I have sealed your inheritance. I have sealed your destiny. I have sealed your future, and your future is secure. I, the Blood, have sealed you forevermore.

HEBREWS 9:13,14

13 For if the blood of bulls and of goats, and the ashes of an heifer sprinkling the unclean, sanctifieth to the purifying of the flesh:

14 How much more shall the blood of Christ, who through the
    eternal Spirit offered himself without spot to God, purge
    your conscience from dead works to serve the living God?

I am the Blood of Renewal. I purge your thoughts
and memories. I say you can now move beyond
failures and mistakes. I say you are no longer the
prisoner of sin. And when you fall, you'll hear Me
say, "Get up!" again (and again, and again...)!

I am the Blood of Hope. I say you have a hope
and a future. You have nothing to dread. Things
will mend. I say you have a future of peace, and
not of evil, to give you an expected end.

HEBREWS 11:28

28 Through faith he [Moses] kept the passover, and the sprin-
    kling of blood, lest he that destroyed the firstborn should
    touch them.

I am the Blood of Sprinkling. I say to the
destroyer, you shall not come here. I say to the
plague, you cannot come nigh this dwelling. I say
to the pestilence and storm, this child of God is
under My protection. Be gone!

I am the Blood of the Passover. I call out, "This
one fears God." The Blood of the Lamb has been
applied above this dwelling's door. Evil cannot
enter this place. Shout with Me: Sickness, pass
over! Poverty, pass over! Death, pass over!

HEBREWS 10:19

19 Having therefore, brethren, boldness to enter into the holiest by the blood of Jesus.

I am the Blood of Boldness. By Me you can speak boldly. By Me you can preach boldly, pray boldly, and live boldly. Boldly declare who you are, whose you are, what you have, and what you can do by My virtue. You have a right to enjoy God's highest and best, both now and always. Be bold!

I am the Blood of Courage. I am the cure for the spirit of fear. I empower the righteous to be as bold as lions and to do great exploits. I say with Me in your life, you shall go up at once and possess the land.

I am the Blood of Confidence. I boldly invite you to come into the presence of your Father. Do not be timid. Come and be blessed. Come and be refreshed. Come and find rest. You are welcome to come into your Father's house (you are His next of kin). Enter into the joy of the Lord. Come in.

GENESIS 4:10,11

10 And he said, What hast thou done? the voice of thy brother's blood crieth unto me from the ground.

11 And now art thou cursed from the earth, which hath opened her mouth to receive thy brother's blood from thy hand.

I am the Blood that Speaks. God listens to Me. He hears Me. I speak of unmerited favor and grace. I, the Blood of the Lamb, speak unto God on your behalf. By Me He is persuaded.

I am the Blood of Pleading. Abel's blood cried out for justice, eye for eye, life for life. But I plead for tender mercies, unmerited favor, and unlimited grace. Be at peace. I'm the Blood of Jesus, and right now I'm pleading your case.

THE SANGUINE SONG
By *Larry Huggins*

I was speaking to you, alone.
Yes, even in the crowd.

Sometimes I spoke silently.
Sometimes I spoke aloud.

What I said made you smile
When you wore a frown.

That was Me saying, "Get up!"
When you were cast down.

I said, "Child be humble,"
When you were talking proud.

Sometimes speaking silently.
Sometimes speaking aloud.

When you were weak, said I,
"Let the weak say I'm strong!"

I whispered, "It is well,"
When things seemed all wrong.

Ever from God's altar, hear My cry,
"The final sacrifice!"

"For each and every sin atoned.
I have paid the price."

Through the Word I yet speak,
And I speak as you pray.

Oh, yes, it's true, Child,
The Blood Still Speaks today!

Endnotes

Chapter 1

[1] W. E. Vine, *Vine's Complete Expository Dictionary of Old and New Testament Words* (Nashville: Thomas Nelson, Inc.: 1985) "An Expository Dictionary of New Testament Words," p. 551, s.v. "scourge," "B. Verbs. 1."

[2] Vine, New Testament, p. 551, s.v. "SCOURGE," "B. Verbs. 2": "*Note:* The Jewish method of 'scourging,' as described in the Mishna, was by the use of three thongs of leather, the offender receiving thirteen stripes on the bare breast and thirteen on each shoulder, the 'forty stripes save one,' as administered to Paul five times (2 Cor. 11:24)."

[3] Jake Page and editors of U.S. News Books, eds., *Blood, the River of Life*, vol. 2, *The Human Body Series* (Washington D.C.: U.S. News Books, 1981) p. 7.

[4] Page, *Blood, the River of Life,* p. 56.

[5] James Strong, "Hebrew and Chaldee Dictionary" in *Biblesoft's New Exhaustive Strong's Numbers and Concordance with Expanded Greek-Hebrew Dictionary* electronic database (copyright © 1994 by Biblesoft and International Bible Translators, Inc.) entry #120 from #119, s.v. "Adam," Gen. 2:19.

[6] See John 5:26; 1 John 5:11.

[7] See Psalm 8:4-8; 1 Corinthians 15:45-49.

Chapter 2

[1] See Romans 5:12-15.

[2] See Romans 5:14.

[3] See 1 John 1:7.

[4] Genesis 5:5.

[5] Hebrews 10:5.

[6] See Psalm 90:10; Exodus 15:26.

[7] Mark 15:25,34-37.

[8] See 1 Peter 1:18-19,23.

Chapter 3

1 See John 6:53-56.

2 See 1 Peter 2:24.

3 John 8:32.

4 Romans 8:2.

5 "Greek Dictionary of the New Testament" in *Biblesoft's Strong's,* entry #2638 from #2596 and #2983, s.v. "comprehended," John 1:5.

6 "Hebrew and Chaldee Dictionary" in *Biblesoft's Strong's,* entry #216," from "215," s.v. "light," Gen. 1:3.

7 Ephesians 6:14.

8 Ephesians 6:15.

9 "Greek Dictionary of the New Testament" in *Biblesoft's Strong's,* entry #629, s.v. "redemption," Col. 1:14.

10 Monsignor Ronald Knox, trans., *The Holy Bible: A Translation from the Latin Vulgate in the Light of the Greek and Hebrew Originals* (New York: Sheed and Ward, Inc., 1954 with the permission of the Cardinal Archbishiop of Westminster and Burns and Oates, Ltd.).

11 Matthew 25:41; 2 Peter 2:4; Jude 1:6; Revelation 12:7-9.

Chapter 4

1 See Revelation 1:18.

2 Robert Lowry, "Christ Arose," in *Logos Hymnal* (Fort Worth: Joyful Music Company, 1984).

3 See John 6:55,56.

4 Romans 3:23.

Chapter 5

1 Exodus 21:24 and 23.

2 Before entering the Holy of Holies once a year, Aaron as high priest was to enter the holy place and wash his flesh in water before putting on the holy garments (Lev. 16:4,24). But purification for all

the priests before they performed duties of ministry in the tabernacle was very important. For example, Aaron and his sons, the other priests, were to wash their hands and feet in the laver before going into the tabernacle of the congregation or when going near the altar to minister a burnt offering to the Lord "that they die not." These statutes were to continue throughout their generations (Exod. 30:18-21).

These ongoing methods of purification were necessary even though Aaron and his sons had originally undergone an extended time of consecration (seven days) to make atonement in order for them to minister to the Lord as priests. After Moses set up, anointed, and consecrated the tabernacle and its furnishings (Exod. 40:1-5,30-32), he washed Aaron and his sons with water and anointed and sprinkled them with anointing oil and blood (Lev. 8:2,6,12,22-24,30,33-35).

[3] Exodus 25:17-22.

[4] Revelation 19:4.

[5] See Revelation 4:4.

[6] See Revelation 4:5-8; Isaiah 6:1-4.

[7] See Revelation 4:5.

[8] Revelation 4:8.

[9] See 1 Corinthians 5:7; John 1:29.

A Prayer of Salvation

If you want to experience the new life that God is offering you through Christ, please pray this prayer aloud:

Heavenly Father, I confess that I need Jesus. I cannot save myself. I ask You to receive me just as I am. I believe that Jesus is the Son of God and Savior of mankind. He came to this earth, as God in the flesh; He was born of a virgin; He lived a sinless life, and He paid for my sins when he was crucified at Calvary. I believe that He conquered death, hell, and the grave; destroyed the works of the devil; was raised from the dead; and then went back into heaven to redeem me with His own blood. Thank You for dealing with me according to the infinite and tender mercies of Jesus. I now plead the blood of Jesus for the forgiveness of my sins and the healing of my spirit, soul, and body. By faith in the Son of God, I believe that I am now forgiven, and I believe that I am now a son of God. Thank You for filling me with Your Holy Spirit and helping me live for Christ every day. Thank You for leading me to a church and a pastor who can help me to know more about Your Word and Your plan for my life. In Jesus' name, amen!

Name:_____ Date _____

Important Information

It's important that you have a partner who can help you with your Christian growth and stand with you in faith. I want to be your partner.

If this book has blessed you, it's important that you write me and share your testimony. Always remember to Give HIM Glory!

If you prayed the prayer of salvation and meant it, you are a child of God. Now you need to learn how to live the Christian life. I've prayed that you will find a Bible-believing church with genuine Christians and an anointed pastor, where you can grow and become fruitful.

God bless and keep you always.

Rev. Larry Huggins / Ambassador

Date _____

Last Name _____

First Name _____

Middle Name _____

E-Mail _____

Phone _____

Title _____

_____ I prayed the prayer for the first time.

_____ I rededicated my life to the Lord.

_____ My testimony is enclosed on a separate sheet
of paper.

About the Author

Rev. Larry Huggins is an ambassador to Mexico, the U.S.A. and the world. He has traveled to thousands of cities in more than fifty-six nations, planting gospel works and holding miracle crusades and seminars.

He and his wife, Loretta, reside in Central Mexico. They have four adult sons and, at this writing, one grandson. Together they operate Larry Huggins World Embassy, Incorporated (aka Ambassador International Ministries, Inc.).

To contact Larry Huggins please write or call:

Ambassador Larry Huggins

Ambassador International Ministries, Inc.

P. O. Box 140645

Austin, TX 78714-0645 USA

1-888-yes-life

*Please include your prayer requests
and comments when you write.*

Books by Larry Huggins

The Blood Speaks
The Cup of Blessing—Sharing Communion as a Family
Available from your
local bookstore.

If this book has been a blessing to you
or if you would like to see more of the
Harrison House product line,
please visit us on our website at
www.harrisonhouse.com

HARRISON HOUSE
Tulsa, Oklahoma 74153

The Harrison House Vision

Proclaiming the truth and the power
Of the Gospel of Jesus Christ
With excellence;

Challenging Christians to
Live victoriously,
Grow spiritually,
Know God intimately.